Moving Liturgy

Moving Liturgy

Dance in Christian Worship
A Step-by-Step Guide

Jane C. Wellford

RESOURCE *Publications* • Eugene, Oregon

MOVING LITURGY
Dance in Christian Worship, A Step-by-Step Guide

Copyright © 2016 Jane C. Wellford. All rights reserved. Except for brief quotations in critical publications or reviews, no part of this book may be reproduced in any manner without prior written permission from the publisher. Write: Permissions, Wipf and Stock Publishers, 199 W. 8th Ave., Suite 3, Eugene, OR 97401.

Resource Publications
An Imprint of Wipf and Stock Publishers
199 W. 8th Ave., Suite 3
Eugene, OR 97401

www.wipfandstock.com

PAPERBACK ISBN: 978-1-4982-3006-3
HARDCOVER ISBN: 978-1-4982-3008-7
EBOOK ISBN: 978-1-4982-3007-0

Manufactured in the U.S.A.

I dedicate this book to the original members of *Moving Liturgy Dance Ensemble*: Anita M. Davis, Ingrid M. Murphy, Ginger Strickland, Betsy Reeves, and Jane C. Wellford, and to the many other dancers who have been a contributing part of this ensemble over the years.

Contents

List of Images | ix
Preface—You Want Me To Dance . . . In Church? | xiii
Acknowledgments | xxi
Introduction | xxiii

Part I—Liturgical Dance: A Background

Chapter 1—What Is Liturgical Dance? | 3
Chapter 2—The Human Body: The Perfect Visual Aid | 16
Chapter 3—Intention in Liturgical Dance | 29

Part II—Laying the Foundation for Liturgical Dance

Chapter 4—The Host Church or Worship Community | 41
Chapter 5—The Director or Choreographer of Liturgical Dance | 50
Chapter 6—Preparation for the Liturgical Dancer | 61
Chapter 7—Where Will the Dance Occur Within the Liturgy? | 66
Chapter 8—Worship Collaboration: Dancers Working with Clergy, Musicians, Readers of Text, and Staff | 74

Contents

Part III—Practical Areas Regarding Liturgical Dance

Chapter 9—Space: Give Those Dancers an Inch and They'll Take an Aisle! | 89

Chapter 10—Costume Suggestions | 105

Chapter 11—Fees: To Charge or Not to Charge? | 115

Chapter 12—How to Create a Liturgical Dance Group for Your Church | 120

Chapter 13—Choreography for Liturgical Dance | 128

Part IV—Shared Experiences of Liturgical Dance

Chapter 14—Interviews with Clergy, Church Musicians, Dancers, Choreographers, and Others Who Have Experienced Liturgical Dance | 165

Part V—Glossaries of Terms

Glossary A. Terms for Liturgical Dance, Spatial Directions, and Dance Categories | 179

Glossary B. Terms for Church Music | 187

Glossary C. Terms for Church Sanctuary Spaces | 190

Glossary D. Terms for Christian Worship and Church Personnel | 193

Bibliography | 197

Images

Chapter 1

1. *Praise,* Katherine Southard, photo courtesy Elon University | 4
2. *Prayer,* Matthew Baker, photo by Kim Walker | 6
3. *Glory,* Grace Strickland, Lilli Canaday, Kennedy Bennett, photo by John Moran | 10
4. *Hallelujah,* Anita Davis, Ginger Strickland, Ingrid Murphy, Betsy Reeves, photo by Bethany Cubino | 12

Chapter 2

5. *Sharing Another's Burden,* Miles Williams, Sam Eisenstadt, photo by Kim Walker | 18
6. *Division,* Ashley Meerbergen, AmyWagoner, photo by Randy Piland | 21
7. *Assisting,* Ashley Meerbergen, Julie Crothers, photo by Randy Piland | 23
8. *Joy,* Leigh Stanfill, photo by Kim Walker | 25
9. *Fear,* Heather Zachary, photo by Kim Walker | 27

Images

Chapter 3

10. *Asking*, Ingrid Murphy, Betsy Reeves, Anita Davis, photo by Jane Wellford | 33
11. *Three Marys*, Heather Zachary, Fiona Koch, Leigh Stanfill, photo by Kim Walker | 36

Chapter 4

12. *Celebration*, Anita Davis, Ginger Strickland, Jane Wellford, Betsy Reeves, Ingrid M. Murphy, photo by Debbie Lynch | 43
13. *Pentecost*, Anita Davis, Ginger Strickland, Betsy Reeves, Ingrid Murphy, photo by Bethany Cubino | 45

Chapter 5

14. *Peace*, Jane Wellford, photo by Jack Sink | 52
15. *Forgive Us Our Trespasses*, Matthew Baker, Sam Eisenstadt, Miles Williams, photo by Kim Walker | 55
16. *Awakened by Grace*, Leah Palmer, Sarah Beacham, photo by Randy Piland | 58

Chapter 6

17. *Assurance of Pardon*, Fiona Koch, Leigh Stanfill, photo by Kim Baker | 63
18. *Processional Entry*, Betsy Reeves, photo by Kim Walker | 65
19. *Grateful*, Fiona Koch, photo by Kim Walker | 68

Images

Chapter 7

20. *Dance of Gladness*, Grace Stickland, Kennedy Bennett, and others, photo by John Moran | 70
21. *Mother and Child*, Anita Davis, Ingrid Murphy, photo by Jane Wellford | 73

Chapter 8

22. *My Spirit Soars*, Emerson Bennett, photo by Anna Varnadoe | 76
23. *I Am Listening*, Amy Wagoner, photo by Randy Piland | 80

Chapter 9

24. *Macedonia Lutheran Church*, Burlington, NC, photo by Jane Wellford | 91
25. *St. Marks Church*, Burlington, NC, photo by Jane Wellford | 93
26. *First Lutheran Church*, Greensboro, NC, photo by Jane Wellford | 96
27. *St. Andrews-Covenant Presbyterian Church*, Wilmington, NC, photo courtesy Sharon Miller | 97
28. *Elon Community Church*, Elon, NC, photo by Jane Wellford | 101

Chapter 10

29. *Recessional Dance*, Leigh Stanfill, photo by Kim Walker | 107

Images

30. *Teaching the Word*, Betsy Reeves, Ingrid Murphy, Ginger Strickland, Jane Wellford, Anita Davis, photo by Bethany Cubino | 109
31. *Our Father*, Heather Zachary, Fiona Koch, Kaelyn Green, photo by Kim Walker | 112

Chapter 12

32. *United in Prayer*, Sam Eisenstadt, Fiona Koch, Matthew Baker, Leigh Stanfill, Heather Zachary, Kaelyn Green, Miles Williams, Katelyn Smith, photo by Kim Walker | 122
33. *Sharing and Blessing*, Heather Zachary, Katelyn Smith, photo by Kim Walker | 123
34. *Filled with Joy*, Miles Williams, photo by Kim Walker | 125

Chapter 13

35. *Guided by the Star*, Leigh Stanfill, Katelyn Smith, Fiona Koch, photo by Kim Walker | 133
36. *Awe and Majesty*, Anita Davis, Jane Wellford, Ingrid Murphy, Ginger Strickland, Betsy Reeves, photo by Debbie Lynch | 137

PREFACE

You Want *Me* To Dance
  . . . In Church?

(Religious and Artistic Background of the Author)

DOUG ADAMS, PROFESSOR AND author of many books on the subject of liturgical dance, once told me in a phone conversation, "If you write a book on liturgical dance, you should inform the readers of where you are coming from so they will take you seriously." The following is a brief summary of my personal journey as a dancer of the sacred, and why I am compelled to share the *how to* of this extraordinary worship art.

Religious Background

I was raised in the Christian faith as a member of Holy Trinity Lutheran Church in Hickory, North Carolina. Our church was a member of the Evangelical Lutheran Church in America. The religious education I received growing up as a Lutheran was pretty serious business with all of its ritual, reformation history, classical sacred music, and formal structure. From early childhood through high school, I loved it all. Since my church was large, many participatory opportunities were available for its members, and our family of seven took advantage of all of them: Sunday School, Sunday evening youth group, communicants classes prior to

PREFACE—You Want *Me* To Dance . . . In Church?

Confirmation, Vacation Bible School, summer church camp, outreach programs, pageants during Advent and Lent, and of course, choir. Since there were five choirs, I was in one choir after another, from age six through age eighteen, until I left for college.

The quality of our church choir music was excellent. As a choir, we were taught to sing music by Bach, Beethoven, and Handel, among other composers. Our choir directors taught us how to sing collectively as a group, to harmonize, and to read music. This early choral training was an excellent foundation for my later work with choir directors, musicians, and conductors throughout my years as a choreographer in secular and sacred dance. In addition to choir rehearsals, I took private piano lessons for a few years early in life. But since I played by ear and did not enjoy practicing, I was a music teacher's nightmare. I ceased with piano lessons around age ten or eleven but continued in the church choir. The music training I received from both piano and choir embedded itself deeply in my bones and became a strong musical basis upon which I relied throughout my career in dance.

Another strong influence in my religious background and education was one of our excellent pastors, Pastor John L. Yost. Not only was he proficient in preaching, but he had a gift for the dramatic. Pastor Yost made sure we received the word of God through a variety of ways. One year during the season of Lent, Pastor Yost decided to bring the passion story to life by *enacting* the character of each person involved in the life of Christ during his final days. Each night during Holy Week, Pastor Yost would portray a new character in first person, complete with costume. One night, he was Peter; another night, Judas; another night, Jesus himself, until all characters of the Passion Story were represented from a variety of perspectives. I was mesmerized, watching the events from 2,000 years ago unfold as if the scenarios were occurring in the present. The portrayals were vivid depicting the questions, struggles, doubts, and love each of these individuals had for one another. Most importantly, Pastor Yost portrayed the humanity and sensitivity of Jesus and each person close to him. What a gift this was to me as a viewer! For the first time, through the dramatic arts, I

PREFACE—You Want *Me* To Dance . . . In Church?

was able to finally understand and relate to the humanity of Christ. Here it was, during a Lenten Holy Week service, the incarnation of the Word made flesh, beautifully enacted for me in an artistic presentation. This was one of the strongest epiphanies where my religious education and appreciation of the arts began to intersect into a meaningful whole. I finally began to understand God more fully through a closer relatedness of the humanity of Jesus. My hunger for further theological understanding and knowledge began to grow immeasurably. I continued to be involved in many of our Christmas and Lenten programs in choir and drama opportunities throughout my junior and senior high school years.

In addition to religious educational opportunities provided by my church, during high school I was also involved in Young Life, a national Christian fellowship organization for youth. This was a wonderful complement to my faith journey and provided another safe haven and venue to study scriptures, celebrate, and even vent questions about my faith with other teenagers of like mind.

It was not until my undergraduate studies at St. Andrews Presbyterian College in Laurinburg, North Carolina that I began to really question my faith. During my first year and perhaps into my second year, I became a *seeker*, almost losing my religious foundational education altogether. I took courses in World Religions, as well as Christianity and Cultures, which enlightened me to many other religions and philosophical practices in various cultures. Somewhere during the end of my junior year, I returned to embrace the Christian faith, stronger in my commitment than ever. Bible studies resumed and I met my "husband-to-be" through common interests in athletics and Bible study groups. I completed my Bachelor of Arts in Theatre, and a year and a half after college Randy Wellford and I were married. We lived on the campus of Louisville Presbyterian Theological Seminary in Louisville, Kentucky, where he pursued his Masters of Divinity in Theology and I worked during the day. In the evenings, I took some theology classes at the Southern Baptist Theological Seminary across the street. The Presbyterian Seminary did not offer evening classes

PREFACE—You Want *Me* To Dance . . . In Church?

during this time, and I wanted to feed my continued interest in theology. It was a great post graduate time of learning for us both.

Artistic Background

From age nine through the present, I have been a serious student and performer of dance, trained in ballet, pointe, modern, jazz, and tap. After school each day, I would attend dance classes and be heavily involved in rehearsals and performances on weekends. Countless dance recitals and festival concerts over the years provided numerous performance opportunities. By age twenty-six, I had become a member of three dance companies and was nearing completion of my Master of Fine Arts in Dance at The University of North Carolina at Greensboro. It was during the final semester in graduate school that it happened.

After a dance history class one morning, one of my professors, Dr. Lois Andreason, approached me with an invitation. "A Presbyterian minister in a church in Asheboro, North Carolina, would like for one of our graduate students to choreograph and perform something with the youth of his church for an Easter service. Since you are a dancer *and* a Presbyterian minister's wife, I was wondering if you would be interested." Well, of course I said "Yes." But after she left the room, I became terrified! What was I thinking? I had never seen sacred dance or liturgical dance within worship, except for *The Lord's Prayer* once or twice. Who was I to know what to do? If I screwed up, it might be blasphemous! I might be excommunicated from the church or something! Well, it did give me pause for thought.

Research became my new middle name . . . Jane "research the heck out of liturgical dance" Wellford. Anything that had to do with dancing in church, sacred dance, or liturgical dance, I explored. My research took me to The University of North Carolina at Greensboro's library, Duke University's library, large church libraries, public libraries, the internet, workshops, and many interviews. I took liturgical dance workshops from Doug Adams, Carla de Sola, and other liturgical dance leaders who I knew would give me

PREFACE—You Want *Me* To Dance . . . In Church?

great mentorship in this field. I left no stone unturned. My appetite to know more about dance in worship was voracious. I talked with ministers and dancers anywhere and everywhere. I needed more resources if I was to enter into this new arena of combining dance and worship, two areas I knew a great deal about, but not in combination. Who was I to actually combine these two areas into one form, two areas that were so much a part of my life, but up to this point, housed in two different camps? As I began my research, I discovered dance was primarily sacred in its origins, not only in Christianity, but in many religions throughout the world and throughout history. My pulse began to beat at a more regular pace now. Dance was often born and raised in sacred settings. Ahhh. I felt better.

Most of my early research initially was from sources in both dance history and early liturgical dance by such authors as Margaret Fisk Taylor Doane, Curt Sachs, Agnes De Mille, and Doug Adams. I am most grateful for their research and documentation that helped set me on my path of passion for dancing the sacred. Later, Carla De Sola, Carolyn Deitering, Judith Rock, Diane Apostolos-Cappadona, Constance Fisher, Cynthia Winton-Henry, Phil Porter, Robert VerEecke, Ronald Gagne, Kathleen Cline-Chesson, and Thomas Kane became people I admired for their research, experiences, and writings. Other authors, who are not dancers but writers on matters of faith, spirituality, and social justice who have influenced me to continue in my artistic and theological pursuits, are Tim Hansel, Sam Keen, Anne Valley-Fox, Madeline L'Engle, and Jim Wallis.

That first opportunity for dance in worship at The First Presbyterian Church in Asheboro, North Carolina, was a positive one for everyone involved. My first liturgical choreographed works were a simple Easter hymn for a group of young children and a solo I performed to an Easter anthem sung by the choir. From that first opportunity of dancing in worship, I was transformed. This combination of dance and worship hit me like a mighty "Yes!" This experience felt so right, so worshipful, and so natural to my very

PREFACE—You Want *Me* To Dance ... In Church?

core. I have continued to say *yes* to every opportunity to share liturgical dance from that first experience to the present.

After completion of my Master of Fine Arts in Dance, I became a college professor at Elon University, where I taught dance technique, dance history, dance improvisation, choreography, sacred dance, dance pedagogy, and dance and gender. Prior to and many years during my teaching career, I was a performer of ballet, modern dance, and liturgical dance. I served several years in roles as Dance Mistress, Choreographer, and Artistic Director for a civic company and performed in a professional company. During several of my years at Elon University, I was Dance Coordinator of the Bachelor of Arts Dance Program. In my last ten years at the university, our Performing Arts Department brought in a new Coordinator of Dance who led our dance program into a vibrant future with a new Bachelor of Fine Arts in Dance Performance and Choreography as well as a Bachelor of Science in Dance Science.

It was during my earlier years at Elon University that I became a solo performer of liturgical dance in the community and around the state of North Carolina. After dancing as a solo liturgical dance artist for five years, I decided to create what is now Moving Liturgy Dance Ensemble, now in its twenty-eighth year. After all, several liturgical dancers were more powerful than one, and the creative possibilities were endless. I asked some of my dancing friends with whom I had performed over the years if they were interested. They said *yes* and Moving Liturgy Dance Ensemble was born.

During my full-time career at Elon University, I often tried to leave out the addition of liturgical and sacred dance in my already busy life of teaching, choreographing, performing, and directing for the university and the community at large. The addition of my professional liturgical dance troupe seemed to tip the scale from time to time while I balanced raising my two children, being a minister's wife, and keeping my professional career strong. Why would I want to complicate things further by including this *worship dance* in my life?

Like receiving *the call* to the ministry for those who pursue this career, I felt called to liturgical dance. Liturgical dance is, and

PREFACE—You Want *Me* To Dance . . . In Church?

has been for years, my spiritual worship. Much like the Old Testament prophets, I felt nudged by God and set on the path of liturgical dance. The more I choreograph and create visual tapestries of the Christian faith, the stronger my faith becomes. It is in the shared experience of assisting congregations in a fresh seeing of the word and acting as a catalyst for others in worship that I feel closest to God. When I analyze sacred texts for choreography, perform the sacred texts to music or spoken text, or witness liturgical or sacred dance, I feel I am truly in communion with the Holy.

Over the years, an amazing amount of artistry has been shared and produced by *Moving Liturgy Dance Ensemble*, from exhilarating epiphanies to humbling tearful experiences. According to Albert Einstein, "Imagination is more important than knowledge." There is never a shortage of imaginative ideas from any of our company members. One of our dancers, Betsy Reeves, often reminds us of another Einstein quote: "The measure of intelligence is the ability to change." Both of these quotes have resounded deeply with *Moving Liturgy* over time. When matters of religion and dance are combined, sparks, revelations, surprises, and unexplainable events of amazing proportion are bound to occur. We discovered that, even though we are an extremely imaginative group with years of professional experience among us, we are often challenged by our collaborative work with church personnel and with church architecture. Alternative changes and creative adaptations often had to be made. People are variables, church architecture is not. We have learned humility, adaptability, and strengths as we have together experienced deep joy and high celebration in our worship experiences over time.

Although from varying denominations, all members of *Moving Liturgy* are of the Christian faith. Our mission is to share and reflect God's unconditional love and amazing grace through dance, our spiritual worship. Through physical embodiment of the stories of the Christian faith, our aim is for people to see the God's word afresh. Our years of combined technical training in ballet, modern, contemporary dance, jazz, and theatre provide our avenues through which we share our classical and contemporary choreography using both text and music. At times our dances are humorous, celebrative, and even satirical. Other times, our dances are reflective and introspective. Our goal is to be prophetic, thought-provoking, and worship-enhancing on a variety of levels. We have been privileged to share our dances of worship all over the United States in more than seven hundred churches, numerous arts festivals, and national conferences.

As performing artists of *Moving Liturgy* and long-time friends, we realize we have been gifted with the ability to dance for some reason. Using our gifts of dance as a ministry has been a commitment of love and artistry, as well as countless years of hard work with great support from our families. A bond of closeness has grown over the years that has been stronger than any knee injuries or strained backs we have incurred during our time together.

It was a combination of all of these things in my early years that fertilized the soil for my future in religion and the arts. My religious education from church, early artistic training in dance and music, and a loving and supportive family were better than any Miracle Grow. For these fertilizers to the soil of my early years, I am grateful. These experiences laid the foundation for the path on which I continue today as both a liturgical dancer and an advocate of all sacred dance.

For more than thirty years, I have been actively involved in the choreography and teaching of liturgical and sacred dance. One of my favorite university courses I continue to teach is *Dance in Worship: How Dance and Gesture are used in World Religions.*

Acknowledgments

WITH LOVE AND GRATITUDE, I would like to thank my wonderful family: Randolph T. Wellford, my husband and great encourager, who was unfailing with his patience and confidence in me throughout the writing of this book. I thank my children, Eric and Whitney Wellford, who as young children, sat through many long rehearsals in churches often working as my sound technicians.

I am deeply appreciative to the following people for their invaluable peer review reading and editing contributions with this book, making it far richer for their insights and assistance: Rev. Richard McBride, Dr. Karen Josephson, J. Patrick Murphy, Cynthia Winton-Henry, Wendy Morrell, Betsy Reeves, Vicky Wilder, Mary Kamp, David VanderMeer, and David Ratchford.

I wish to thank my copyeditors Jane Gwinn, Linda Martindale, and Lauren Phillips for their time and attention to detail throughout the process. I am very grateful to Jean Taylor who encouraged me and taught me layout options and aesthetic possibilities for this book.

Finally, I wish to thank the students from Elon University Elite Technology Services for their assistance and support with my numerous computer questions throughout my final typing stages, in particular Samantha Allen.

Introduction

THIS BOOK IS WRITTEN is for dancers, non-dancers, and *everyone* who is open to new ways of seeing and/or experiencing worship through movement, gesture, and dance on small to grand scales. It is filled with tried and true experiences of a dance troupe who has actively collaborated with clergy, musicians, laity, and other artists in churches and conferences for many years. The stories I share are often humorous because I think it is important to share both mistakes as well as joys for learning purposes. Rich and enlightening insights are shared from interviews with clergy, musicians, dancers, and others who offer heartfelt commentary from experiencing liturgical dance in their congregations, at conferences, or other worship venues.

As you journey through this book, notice there are four helpful glossaries of terms in the back of this book to assist with any explanations you may require regarding terms for dance, church music, sanctuary spaces, worship liturgy, and church personnel. Many terms throughout the chapters are in italics to remind the reader they are defined in the glossaries.

A chapter with easy to follow choreography is included to share ways to bring prayers, hymns, scriptures, litanies, and parables to life through movement. Spacing dilemmas and solutions are tackled in this book regarding old and new sanctuary settings where information is included with advice regarding potential pitfalls to avoid.

Introduction

In conclusion, I have come to appreciate the profound privilege of being a dancer by profession with the opportunity of using liturgical dance as my spiritual worship. As a liturgical dancer and choreographer, I have often begun my spiritual worship long before my dances are shared within the worship liturgy. It is in the analysis of the text, the study of the music, the creation of the choreography, and the rehearsals that my worship begins. On many occasions I have felt the presence and holiness of God within worship as I have danced joy, sadness, questions, and everything in between. Worship for me occurs within and through both the process and the product of liturgical dance. It is with deepest gratitude that I thank my friends, colleagues, and collaborators for our work together in the creative process of rich and meaningful sacred worship arts.

PART I

Liturgical Dance: A Background

CHAPTER 1

What is Liturgical Dance?

Upon his return from battle with the Philistines, a jubilant King David, the second king of Israel, entered the city of Jerusalem and "danced before the Lord with all his might."[1] "Let them praise his name with dancing," states Psalm 149:3.[2] These are only two of the many scripture examples from *The Holy Bible* mentioning the use of dance as worship. Why do some people feel a need to worship with physical gesture, full body movement, or actual dance? What is all this lifting of arms, swaying, and twirling about in worship? Is it something from our historic past, or a very present and active way to worship today?

Dance is and has been an integral part of worship for numerous world religions and spiritual practices for centuries. One of the ten major purposes for the use of dance in history in many world cultures is the use of dance in worship.[3] Anthropologic studies of early cave and rock paintings from the Mesolithic period record very physical dances of humans dancing in religious or spiritual ritual celebrations.[4] Upon realization of their own mortality and the temporal existence of all living things, pre-historic humans felt a need to reach beyond the *seen* and communicate with deities

---

1. Zondervan, *Holy Bible, New International Version*, II Samuel 5:14, 346.
2. Ibid., Psalm 149:3, 714.
3. Kraus, et al, *History of the Dance in Art and Education*, 22.
4. Kassing, *History of Dance, an Interactive Approach*, 26.

PART I—Liturgical Dance: A Background

and spirits of the *unseen*. The human body was the most basic and immediate instrument through which this communication would first take place.

Praise, Katherine Southard, photo courtesy Elon University.

Although initial movements such as leaps, turns, and uplifted arms were at first rough and unrefined, such movements were the beginning of a way to express, to praise, to question, and to communicate with forces of nature, gods, and spirits. We know from

What is Liturgical Dance?

the early cave paintings that early ritual dances were very physical experiences, not merely cerebral.

Dance is an art form performed by individuals or groups, existing in time and space, and using force and flow, where the human body is the instrument and movement is the medium.[5] *Sacred dance* is dance that is holy, dedicated to a god or spirit, connected with religion or matters of the spirit, set apart for sacred purposes.[6] The term *sacred dance* may be used when speaking about dances of worship in any religious, spiritual, or faith tradition throughout the world.

The word *liturgy* comes from the Greek word *leitourgia* which means "a public work."[7] *Strong's Concordance* additionally defines the word as "a service; a ministry."[8] The earliest meaning of the word was derived from the physical work performed by the community, such as the building or maintaining of roads or buildings for the greater good of the community.[9] Over time, the meaning changed to become "prescribed form of public worship."[10]

Liturgical dance is dance often shared within the worship liturgy by dancers, from novice to professional, for the purpose of worshipping God and bringing those viewing into a closer communion with God. It may occur in various locations other than a church or sanctuary, but its intention and purpose remain the same. Dance within the liturgy may at times be called *sacred dance* when referencing it with the larger body of sacred dances of other world religions. When shared within the liturgy of Christian worship, *sacred dance* is most often called *liturgical dance*.

Liturgical dance often enhances the spoken or sung word and serves as a conduit, a channel or path, to connect worshippers through a fresh seeing of the word. Those worshipping may be drawn into a heightened sense of attention as the visual

---

5. Kraus, et al, *History of the Dance in Art and Education*, 24.
6. Jewell, *Oxford American Desk Dictionary and Thesaurus*, 735.
7. Richardson, *Dictionary of Christian Theology*, 197–198.
8. *Strong's Concordance*, http://biblehub.com/greek/3009.htm
9. Richardson, *Dictionary of Christian Theology*, 197–198.
10. Jewell, *Oxford American Desk Dictionary and Thesaurus*, 485.

part i—Liturgical Dance: A Background

presentation of a liturgical dance takes them to a deeper receptive place beyond the words themselves. The visual worship arts of dance and drama both use the human body as the instrument of performance. It is through this physical embodiment of the word that the worshipping community receives an immediate point of relatedness. In addition to those worshipping, the dancers themselves often receive a heightened worship experience during the sharing of dance or drama as they *embody* or "give discernible form"[11] to the spoken or sung word. Rev. Richard McBride states,

> The power of sacred dance in the Christian faith is that it echoes the opening of John's Gospel: 'And the Word became flesh and dwelt among us, full of grace and truth.' Sacred dance serves the worshipping community by embodying the gospel, teaching that God's grace is the very life that flows through every breath and movement of our being.[12]

Prayer, Matthew Baker, photo by Kim Walker.

---

11. Ibid., 256.
12. McBride, quote from online interview, 2010.

What is Liturgical Dance?

Liturgical dance carries an expectation that it enables others within worship to be more connected to the worship experience, ultimately the congregation's communion with God and one another. Anne Saxon states, "Liturgical dance is truly the externalization of the sacred word; the visual manifestation of scripture in movement."[13] Jeanette Hassell adds, "It is a dramatic stirring of space that quickens the soul and enriches the sacred mindset being sought."[14] Christian liturgical dance is most often based on Judeo-Christian scriptures of the Old and New Testaments of *The Holy Bible*. This is liturgical dance's main springboard, but it certainly does not stop there. Liturgical dance may use other complementary theological texts, musical scores, poetry, or commentaries to expand its thematic options. I will be referencing liturgical dance mainly from the Judeo-Christian historic perspective, as my religious education and ethnographic work has been largely from this base of knowledge and learning. Nina Bryans states,

> If we move from the academic study of theology to the place where the congregation is in worship and mission, we find the arts are so imbedded in the life of the church that we almost have to be reminded of them—architectural space, music and poetry, image, gesture, movement, the way a sermon is preached, the sacraments celebrated, etc.[15]

In Nena Bryans' quote above, five of the arts mentioned as "imbedded in the life of the church" were *music, poetry, image, gesture*, and *movement*. All of these art forms are directly associated with dance in liturgy. Liturgical dance, like other visual worship arts, is primarily intended as an aid to worship, taking on major or minor portions of a worship service. It may be shared by a soloist or a group of dancers who serve as leaders or aids within worship, much like the choir, lay readers, or others leading in worship. At times, the entire congregation or body of worshippers might be dancing within worship.

13. Saxon, quote from online interview, 2010.
14. Hassell, quote from online interview, 2010.
15. Bryans, "Arts in the Church," 2

PART I—Liturgical Dance: A Background

The early Shakers of the eighteenth through twentieth centuries, also known as The United Society of Christ's Second Appearance, used dancing and singing throughout their worship services as their main manner of worship. They would lift their hands high to receive God's spirit, and shake their hands low to shake off the sins of the flesh as they danced in geometric choreographed floor patterns throughout their worship.[16]

A third category of dance, *secular dance*, is "any type of dance performed for self-expression, entertainment, or other purposes; not concerned with religion or religious beliefs; not spiritual or sacred."[17] Therefore, the focus and intention of *liturgical dance* is different from *secular dance*. Even with this distinction being made, there are many times in the viewing of a secular dance where *catalyst imagery* might come into play and cause the viewer of a secular dance to reflect on the Holy. A *catalyst* is "a person or thing that precipitates a change."[18] In *catalyst imagery*, Judith Rock states the viewer might see a dance that could be about anything, where the dance, secular or sacred, may influence the viewer to notice or be inspired toward a theological or spiritual reflection.[19] "The Greeks believed that dance was the art that most influenced the soul and provided the expressive way for that overflow of awareness for which there were no words."[20]

Within the Bible, "there are eleven verb forms to describe dancing."[21] One can easily locate approximately twenty-two different scripture passages within the Bible to document dance, including metaphoric references. "*The Hymn of Jesus* reveals that *symbolic movement* was employed in the second and third centuries."[22] Liturgical dance was practiced with more formal structure in Christian worship as early as the Middle Ages in the

16. Kraus, et al., *History of the Dance in Art and Education*, 106–108.
17. Jewell, *Oxford American Desk Dictionary and Thesaurus*, 754.
18. Ibid., 117.
19. Rock, "Dance, Texts, and Shrines," 188–189.
20. Taylor, "A History of Symbolic Movement in Worship," 16.
21. Gruber, "Ten Dance Derived Expressions in the Hebrew Bible," 48.
22. Taylor, "A History of Symbolic Movement in Worship," 17.

What is Liturgical Dance?

form of both solo and communal dances, communal being preferred over solo dance.[23]

In "Image as Insight," Margaret Miles of Harvard University states, "Until the 16th century, art and religion were interwoven ... In the 16th century, reformers preached against the exaggerated concentration of religious images and the corresponding neglect of religious language."[24] Nena Bryans, from her article *Arts in the Church: A Theological and Pedagogical Rationale*, adds the following:

> This led to a needed correction for that time with an emphasis on 'hearing the Word' and away from anything that might detract from the Word. Four hundred years later, we are in a very different time, but we have not altogether shaken that mind-set of the Reformation.[25]

Throughout history, dance in liturgy could be described much like a revolving door, in and out of the church depending on two things: who was in power in the church and how it was performed or shared. Still today, this often holds true.

"The development of dance as a performance fine art in the Western Christian liturgical context is a twentieth-century phenomenon."[26] Dancers have shared worship dances as early as pre-history in numerous religions of the world. But until the twentieth century in Christian worship, dancers and choreographers were for the most part non-professional, with little or no professional training. Prior to twentieth century, participants of Christian dance in worship were perhaps priests, altar youth, or other members of the worshipping community participating in occasional communal or choral dances. Not until the twentieth century in Europe and parts of America did more *skilled* dancers with technical dance training begin sharing dance within worship. The dance techniques used by these early twentieth century

---

23. Adams, "Communal Dance Forms and Consequences in Biblical Worship," 35.

24. Miles, "Image as Insight," 2.

25. Bryans, "Arts in the Church: A Theological and Pedagogical Rationale," 2.

26. Bauer, "Dance as Performance Fine Art in Liturgy," 167.

PART I—Liturgical Dance: A Background

participants were most likely from ballet training, early modern dance, or gestural pedestrian movements.

Glory, Grace Strickland, Lilli Canaday, Kennedy Bennett, photo by John Moran.

When used within worship liturgy, liturgical dance may be found within any part of the existing worship service, from prayers and sermons to processionals and hymns. Liturgical dance is often shared using music, readings from texts, or within silence. Those worshipping might witness the words literally coming to life through the dancer's visual movements where words, music, or singing are used, thereby giving the viewers a multi-sensory worship experience, visual and auditory. All dance, whether liturgical or secular, is interpretive since crafting a dance is a choreographer's artistic interpretation of what she trying to communicate.

What is Liturgical Dance?

It is not only the choreographer's intention of the liturgical dance, but also what the receptive viewers bring to the experience that affects what is ultimately received.

Liturgical dance within worship is often like a danced prayer. When an individual prays, she is most often sharing a cerebral experience of silence, or a verbal statement, chant, or song when communicating with God. The prayer might be about anything, such as thanksgiving, confession, or questioning. The liturgical dancer externalizes this same type of conversation with God through dance movement and gesture. Upon the viewing of this danced prayer, those witnessing are often able to relate and connect clearly to the dancer's message, whether the dance is literal or abstract. It is no longer the dancer's prayer, but everyone's prayer, the moment it becomes externalized. There is the opportunity to clearly see a glimpse of ourselves in the image of another as we pursue our communication with the Holy. Somehow in the seeing of ourselves through another's shared prayer, there is often a sense of shared commonality.

Around the 1970s, additional dance genres such as jazz, hip hop, tap, ethnic, and mime began to appear in less formal Christian worship locations. Sign language began to be used in worship to enable the hearing impaired more access to understanding worship and the signing movments were often set to music as a beautiful worship art form. These newer worship dance and movement genres, together with the already in place ballet, modern, and contemporary dance, can be further categorized into broad worship dance categories such as *praise dance, reflective dance, interpretive dance, improvisational dance,* and *freestyle dance.* Songs and dances used to tell stories of the Christian faith also began to appear on Broadway and other stage venues in the early 1970s in such musicals as *Jesus Christ Superstar, Godspell,* and *Joseph and the Amazing Technicolor Dreamcoat.*

Although liturgical dance is most often found within the actual worship liturgy during a structured worship setting, liturgical dance may often occur in other locations. Liturgical and sacred dance may be seen in such locations as outdoor festivals, dance

PART I—Liturgical Dance: A Background

recitals, classrooms, fellowship halls, or other informal gathering sites. What was once born in sacred settings is now able to be seen in various and often surprising locations such as downtown city streets, tourist venues, theme parks, concert arenas and most certainly on internet and other social media.

Hallelujah, Anita Davis, Ginger Strickland, Ingrid Murphy, Betsy Reeves, photo by Bethany Cubino.

Project Dance, under the founding and direction of Cheryl Cutlip since 2002, is an organization where dancers, choreographers, and teachers are not afraid to take dances of positive outreach and worship to the streets. Based in New York City, this highly successful organization offers dancers the opportunity to dance their worship witness and "bring hope and healing through the universal language of dance."[27] *Project Dance* often performs on massive street stages in such cities as New York, Brisbane, Hong Kong, Sydney, London, Toronto, Costa Rica, Jerusalem, Manila, Hollywood, Atlanta, Penang, and Singapore. The *Project Dance* website provides the following mission statement.

> *Project Dance* is guided by the principle that dance is valid in three areas: work, worship, and witness. We labor

27. Project Dance, New York, New York, *Project Dance Foundation* internet website, 2014.

What is Liturgical Dance?

to support dancers in every arena including the aspiring and professional dancers, teachers and the growing world of inspirational dance. These concerts bring hope and healing to hearts and offer a positive message to those who attend.[28]

I admire Project Dance for its courage in taking liturgical and sacred dance out of traditional worship settings and placing this type of dance out among the people. John West, Artistic Director of Valyermo Dancers, shares the following quote: "It's easy to dance where people like you and approve you. Where it really is going to challenge you is when you take it to the Philistines."[29] West attributes this quote to Father Vincent Martin, a Belgian Benedictine Monk from St. Andrew's Abby in Valyermo, California in the late 1970's. West continues:

> We need to step outside the safety zone of the welcoming churches and take our work into what others see as the secular world, ergo 'Philistines.' With that in mind, the Valyermo Dancers ventured out into concert work at various universities and into non-ecclesial settings such as high-end shopping plazas and even Dodger Stadium for the visit of Pope John Paul II. All of it meant using dance as an art form to communicate and carry the *sacred* into the outside world.[30]

When used within a service of worship, liturgical dance may be either participatory or vicarious. *Participatory* means that those worshipping may actually take part in the dance, while *vicarious* refers to watching the dancers perform. It depends on the particular worship community and what is being offered in worship whether one style is preferred over another. In a vicarious experience, those worshipping may be called to sit or stand quietly and watch a liturgical dance within worship as they might view a nativity play. The presented dance may be of a serious reflective nature or of advanced technical content, not intended for any

---

28. Ibid.
29. West, Panel Discussion at Sacred Dance Guild, 2003.
30. West, Phone conversation with John West, June, 2015.

PART I—Liturgical Dance: A Background

participatory experience beyond visual and emotional encounter with the dance. On other occasions, a liturgical dance may make available the opportunity for worshippers to be participants in the dance within the service. This participatory liturgical dance experience may often be found at times of communal celebration, church unity, or prayers for peace. Many churches welcome spontaneous dances of worship within worship and see this as both a regular and welcome occurrence. Other churches or worship communities may find this a visual distraction within their worship. It is a personal choice of the worship community and always a good idea for guest liturgical dancers to know protocol ahead of time.

My experiences of sharing dance in worship have been mostly positive and enriching. Being an educator, I have tried to inform the worship community prior to every dance in worship experience about what they will be experiencing, either within the service or in a bulletin insert. As a choreographer, I create liturgical dances often based on scriptures and other sacred texts, in addition to other texts that inspire me. If I choose to use music, it is often sacred, spiritual, classical, contemporary, or perhaps ambient sounds. Often I choreograph to dramatic readings of texts. Like any artist, my created works are interpretations. Through prayer, analysis, and research I bring the spoken or sung words to life through movement. My own worship begins early within the process, long before the dance has come to fruition. The lens through which I interpret is fairly broad since my dances range from literal to abstract. My liturgical dances are sometimes "easy on the eye" and quite lovely. But at other times my works might be difficult to watch, as they may depict the harsh realities of social injustice. Not all liturgical dance is "beautiful and flowing," as some of my students tend to label most liturgical dance before further education.

Regardless of the many genres used to create and share liturgical dance, it must be handled with care when shared with any worshipping community. The human body is a fragile yet powerful instrument, "the crowning glory of God's creation in Genesis."[31] When used effectively, liturgical dance and many forms of sacred

---

31. Kline-Chesson, "The Living Word: Dance as a Language of Faith," 314.

What is Liturgical Dance?

dance, can be one of the most profound and creative tools we have to heighten our worship and commune with the Holy. Ronald Gagne's words sum up this chapter beautifully in the following ending quote.

> The future importance of dance and the use of other gestures, postures, and actions in the liturgy lies in the fact that they can encourage us to become more aware of the visual and tactile senses as vehicles of God's powerful presence in our daily lives.[32]

---

32. Gagne, "The Place of Movement in the Liturgical Prayer of Today," 70.

CHAPTER 2

The Human Body: The Perfect Visual Aid

WHAT DOES IT MEAN to be a *visual aid* in worship? How can a dancer as a visual aid portray stories about the knowledge and teachings of a faith practice through dance? Can we portray the miracles of God, the sacredness of life, and the wonders of creation with the instrument of our bodies? Can we be prophetic in our visual dances about justice and peacemaking?

One of the most unique characteristics about Christianity is that it is a faith of *incarnation*, "embodiment in human flesh."[1] "The Word became flesh and dwelt among us," from John 1:14 in *The Bible*, references the physical birth of God's son, Jesus. Within the Old Testament scriptures, numerous prophets foretold the birth of Jesus years before the actual event. The scriptures were fulfilled when God indeed did send this most perfect gift to humankind, Jesus, God's *visual aid*.

As mentioned in chapter 1, to *embody* means "to give a concrete or discernible form to an idea, or concept of a thing or person; to be an expression of an idea."[2] *The Oxford American Dictionary* continues to include synonyms for *embody* such as "realize, materialize, manifest, express, personify, demonstrate, epitomize."[3]

---

1. Jewell, *Oxford American Desk Dictionary and Thesaurus*, 412.
2. Ibid., 256.
3. Ibid., 256.

The Human Body: The Perfect Visual Aid

When we hear *embodiment of the word*, we often begin to process images in our mind. If the words we hear spoken or sung in worship lead us to visual imagery, we might say, "that really helped me embody my understanding of the message." However, if we are given a visual aid of the human body within worship in addition to the spoken or sung word, the intended message can be implicitly clearer. This is easily achieved with visual arts in worship such as liturgical dance. James B. Nelson writes, "The body can be word itself... the Word made flesh... Christian faith is an incarnational faith, a faith in the repeatable and continuing incarnation of God. God is uniquely known to us through human presence, and human presence is always embodied presence."[4]

Because the instrument for the choreographer of liturgical dance is the human body, and the incarnation of God was made manifest in human form in Jesus, the Christ, what better instrument is there to reflect God than the human body? Could it be any more direct? On a dancer's body, the choreographer can easily portray Christ's teachings, but also the joys and struggles we all have in common with his humanity. There is a sense of immediacy and clarity when worshippers have a visual aid like the human body to see the stories of the Christian faith. This visual *imagery* enables the viewer an immediate visual and "mental representation."[5] In liturgical dance, this imagery could be a metaphoric or actual image that more clearly captures the viewer's understanding for the prayer, hymn, or text being conveyed through dance.

If the human body is the instrument for liturgical dance in worship, and worship is our communion with the Holy, do we sometimes feel unworthy using our physical bodies as the conduit for worship? Our bodies are what we live in, laugh in, work in, and play in. We carry out our mundane and sometimes profane daily functions within these bodies. Can we also worship with these same bodies? My answer is a resounding, *yes*!

---

4. Nelson, "Embodiment: An approach to Sexuality and Christian Theology," 35-36

5. Jewell, *Oxford American Desk Dictionary and Thesaurus*, 403.

PART I—Liturgical Dance: A Background

Sharing Another's Burden, Miles Williams and Sam Eisenstadt, photo by Kim Walker.

From Genesis 1:27 in *The Bible,* "God created man in his own image, in the image of God he created him; male and female he created them." As a choreographer, the opportunity to choreograph the life of Christ and the miracles of God from the scriptures is such a profound privilege. The analysis, the choreographic process, the teaching, the rehearsal, and the sharing are all my practice of spiritual worship.

The Human Body: The Perfect Visual Aid

When an artist is inspired, there is the opportunity to create something far beyond the artist's potential. In her article, "Full of Grace and Truth," Kari Jo Verhulst writes,

> Painters, writers, musicians, and dancers remind us that faith, like art, must be equal part sweat and release, struggle and letting go . . . Somewhere, between the blinding light of Christ and the darkness of human despair, the artist lets go, and truth takes flight. Then the created—the song, the mural, the essay—brings forth a life force much greater than its human creator, something of God that upon being heard or seen or read culls forth a great sign of recognition, an utterly human 'yes, that is how it is' that makes walking this path more joyful, less lonely, and more possible.[6]

When those worshipping see the miracles of God and the teachings of Christ enacted through dance or drama, powerful messages are communicated that are unforgettable. The message is reinforced because it is a multi-sensory sharing of information—seeing *and* hearing of the word on the human body—the perfect visual aid to embody the incarnation.

As an artist in the field of education, I am ever aware of the diversity of learning styles. In my office, I have this quote posted on the wall as a reminder of how people retain information.

> *Memory: We retain . . .*
>
> 10 percent of what we read
> 20 percent of what we hear
> 30 percent of what we see
> 50 percent of what we hear and see
> 70 percent of what we say
> 90 percent of what we say and do.[7]

Advances in education, technology, and the recognition of different learning styles have caused many churches to change their worship trends. Multi-sensory learning is learning that

---

6. Verhulst, *Full of Grace and Truth: The Power of God in the Creative Vocation*, 16-18.

7. Chinese Proverb attributed to Confucius

Part I—Liturgical Dance: A Background

occurs through the use of a variety of sensory experiences. The possibilities for visible, audible, tactile, and experiential ways to worship are available today for those who wish to use them. If we are serious about effective communication in worship, why not shoot for at least 50 percent retention as opposed to the often 20 percent in worship? We do have options.

Are we doing all we can to keep worship alive today? Are we inspired, changed, or even reflective when we leave worship? Do we always get the message? I believe that worship should be made as multi-sensory, vibrant, and as connected to real life experiences as possible. The more senses that are involved in worship, the more likely the message will be received. There is simply a higher success rate of retention. When we can *hear* the word of God through words or music, *see* it come to life through dance, drama, or other visual arts, *experience* it through speaking the prayers, confessions, or creeds, and *sing* it through hymns or chants, we are more actively engaged in the experience of worship.

If the occasion arises for a specified group of dancers to share a liturgical *danced message* with those watching and receiving in worship, the dancers need to be acutely aware of their responsibilities as leaders in worship reflecting God's word to others. As embodiment of the word of God through dance and gesture, dancer's movements must be well-rehearsed with clear focus. Time and attention must be given to analysis of the presented scriptural text or song through movement for the message being portrayed to be understood by the group of dancers who are sharing. Appropriate focus, technique, emotion, costuming, and other presentation elements all need careful attention prior to sharing with the worshipping community. However, if there is a liturgical dance opportunity where *everyone* present in worship is dancing together or separately, and there is no specific group of dancers with a leadership role or specific choreography, then the above suggestions for accuracy and leadership responsibility may not apply.

The Human Body: The Perfect Visual Aid

Division, Ashley Meerbergen and Amy Wagoner,
photo by Randy Piland.

In creating a dance of worship to be used within the liturgy, I continually put myself in the position of those who will be receiving the dance, the congregation or worshipping community. It is never a one-way street from only the dancer's perspective. As I sit in the sanctuary during rehearsals, I become the viewer and ask these questions: Is the intended message clearly communicated? How can the movements be clarified to be more specific? Is the dancer's focus and expression clear?

Within my choreography, I most often communicate through the dance styles of modern dance, contemporary dance, ballet, and pedestrian movement. Since ballet is older and more established as a dance genre or style associated with more classical training, I will elaborate more on my reasons for the use of the style of modern dance. Doug Adams and Judith Rock state, "Modern dance began as a prophetic form in that its purpose was the communication of personal authentic experiences by means of new symbols, new forms, and new ways of moving."[8] In her early modern dance writings, dance critic Selma Jean Cohen adds, "The modern dance is always concerned with the unacceptable symbol, the one that

---

8. Adams and Rock, *Biblical Criteria in Dance: Modern Dance as Prophetic Form*, 85

PART I—Liturgical Dance: A Background

startles us into awareness. The pressure may be subtle or it may be obvious, but it is always there."[9] Doug Adams and Judith Rock continue,

> The early modern dances of Graham, Wigman, and Humphrey did not contemplate eternal ideas but looked at persons in human situations and told the brusque, undecorated, unlovely truth as they saw it. Those choreographers offered us dances that lift up the ambiguity, the humor, the sorrow, the absurdity, and through these realities the truth to be found in ordinary human experience. This lifting up of things as they are is part of the prophetic voice and biblical touchstone within modern dance.[10]

Dances that call us to time and place, call us to question, and hopefully provoke invitation to action for service are the ones I try my hardest to create for Christian worship communities and beyond. The end results are often beautiful and arresting, and at other times harsh, satiric, or confrontational. The choreographic outcome depends on a variety of circumstances: the maturity and technical ability of the available dancers, the worship community's prior experience witnessing liturgical dance, and what the particular invitation and church season might be in which the dancer is invited to participate.

Choreography and dance are always about communication, and communication should always be reciprocal. Otherwise, it's just another lecture. Unless the lecturer is an extremely gifted and animated speaker, the lecture method is one of the weakest methods to teach a subject having only a 20 percent retention of what one hears, while the retention rate of what one hears *and* sees if 50 percent. If we are serious about having worshippers retain what is offered within worship, we might challenge ourselves to use more multi-sensory worship practices to make worship something that is visible, audible, oral, and as often as possible, *do-able*.

9. Cohen, *Modern Dance: Seven Statements of Belief*, 14

10. Adams and Rock, *Biblical Criteria in Dance: Modern Dance as Prophetic Form*, 85

The Human Body: The Perfect Visual Aid

Liturgical dance in worship has the opportunity to be a perfect visual aid for both the dancers through their embodiment and for those receiving this medium as visual enhancement. Just as the stained glass windows were a way to visually see *The Bible* in story pictures in cathedrals since the middle-ages, so also is dance in worship a visual tapestry of images of faith today. Whether dancing the more narrative embodiment of the teachings of Christ, or the abstract essence of God's power through wind and flames at Pentecost, dance and drama in worship provide a way to assist in connecting our relatedness to one another and our communion with the Holy.

Assisting, Ashley Meerbergen and Julie Crothers, photo by Randy Piland.

Acknowledgements of Witnessing the Human Body as an Instrument of Worship

The following are comments from Elon University students, males and females, ages eighteen to twenty-two, after creating and sharing their personal sacred dances on the final class day of Dance in Worship, a General Studies course. Ninety percent of the class had never had a dance class before. Permission was given by each student to share these quotes with you in this book.

PART I—Liturgical Dance: A Background

Christian Hansen, class of 2012—"The beauty of liturgical dance is that it is a living and breathing representation of what God is doing in our lives. Scripture, a given reading, or a specific song is no longer simply words on a page, but it is brought to life and shown in a new light. This is because we are different people, interpreting the words through our own life stories."

Jay Brown, class of 2012—"Dance in worship taught me to connect my body to worship instead of just my mind. Having a visual presentation along with the auditory message really makes worshipping easier for everyone and more powerful.

Courtney Kennedy Taylor, class of 2004—"To be quite honest, when I entered this class, I was not a huge fan of dance. I thought it looked pretty and impressive, and I had a lot of respect for those who are gifted dancers. Beyond that, dance had little meaning in my life. Today, however, was the culmination of a complete 180 degree change in my perspective. To see my classmates, dancers and non-dancers alike, allowing themselves to be vulnerable, reverent, afraid, joyful, powerful, and humble, was moving beyond words. Dance suddenly had significance besides being pretty or impressive. Dance became my connection to my classmates and my connection to a fresh perspective of my faith. The movements became prayers, testimonies, and pleas which filled the room like fragrance from incense, raising our offerings to the Lord. After watching my classmates dance, and having the opportunity to worship alongside them, I feel as though I know their hearts. Some of us expressed a brokenness for the lost, others a burden for the enslaved, and yet others, an overpowering joy found in redemption. All of our life stories, beliefs, passions and convictions made our dances individual and unique. Yet despite the differences, we all had one goal: worship. We all stepped forth in one accord to lay our lives before the One who created us."

Caitlyn Frohring, class of 2015—"The ability to move others is why dancing in worship is so important. We are able to connect with others without speaking and the movements say it all. You must be able to tell the truth through your movements to create a real connection. When a dancer smiled, I felt hope and joy. When

The Human Body: The Perfect Visual Aid

a dancer put his/her head down, I felt a pang of sadness. Creating and performing these dances of worship has connected us as a class because we shared our honesty and support.

Andrew Cafarella, class of 2014—"For me personally, I received just as much out of seeing the dances performed today as I did actually performing my own. The passion, focus, and connection between the dancer and the song's melody or the poem's lyrics were truly phenomenal. Viewing these dances showed me that faith has many forms. The ability of someone to become one with a song, verse, or poem, and use movement to convey or profess their feelings to that piece, is remarkable. Reading, listening, and praying, the mental aspects of faith, can only take one so far. The physical aspect of worship is just as important in showing one's faith. Through dance, we can praise, ask for help, be thankful, or overcome. Each of these songs shared through dance today showed me just that."

Joy, Leigh Stanfill, photo by Kim Walker.

C. Kyle Edwards, class of 2005—"I was truly shocked by all the dances performed today. We have such inspired and talented people in our class. The passion I felt by all the dances was simply overwhelming. Words cannot describe the true beauty I just witnessed today. Without question, God was present today. I found part of myself I didn't know existed."

Megan Kenny, class of 2005—"I only looked at sacred dance as having to do with worship or religion. I never looked at it as having a chance to reveal something about oneself. Worship isn't something that only happens in a church. It is something that happens everywhere, and these dances really showed that. One of the dances I saw today was a dance revealing not only that God is among us and the praise we feel for Him, but also revealing into who we are. It was a dance of worship to me because the dancers were showing how God affects us in everyday life and how He is always with us."

Caroline Rushmore, class of 2015—"After watching the dance choreographed to the *Serenity Prayer* attributed to Reinhold Niebuhr, I noticed the dancers' movements really reflected the spirit of the prayer and made the prayer so much stronger and more powerful. I felt like I really understood the prayer more fully after the dancers' interpretation, which gave the poem greater meaning."

Katherine Saffelle, class of 2012—"I have never worshipped using my body before, but I realized it is my favorite way to be involved in worship. I feel closer and more connected to God after dancing *The Lord's Prayer* and *Amazing Grace*, and it is these moments that made me realize that God is present in life."

Brandi Little Hobbs, class of 2004—"What a gift our bodies are! Sometimes our words just aren't enough to reach the Divine. When we use all the gifts we have been given of mind, body, and spirit, what we create is truly greater than who we are, for God is in it and helps make it whole."

Miles Williams, class of 2015—"Everyone's dance was different and special. It was evident that all of us put thought and effort into each song choice, gesture, and movement. While viewing some of the dances of my classmates, I felt myself smiling and could not control it. In others, I felt the pain and sadness the dance was trying to evoke and realized I was looking at the piece with a totally different lens than before taking this course. For me, being able to enjoy the embodiment of the word really came to life through the dances of worship of my classmates, a tool that I plan to carry with me for the rest of my life."

Fear, Heather Zachary, photo by Kim Walker.

Graham Masell, class of 2005—"Dance is a very vulnerable art form. I really enjoyed the opportunity to reflect on matters of the soul and spirituality."

Taylor Geslak, class of 2015—"Each dance left a large impact on me. From the gracefulness of each performer to the focus on everyone's faces, the dances left a lasting impression on me for hours after the dances ended. I liked how even though we all took the same class, when given the opportunity to choreograph our own dances, each individual looked at that assignment a bit differently. Another aspect I liked about the dances was the music. While some used scripture or religious songs, others chose songs that didn't necessarily have to do with religion, but when paired with the movements, those watching saw it as worship."

PART I—Liturgical Dance: A Background

Rose Allensworth Marsh, class of 2005—"One dance we performed that I see as prophetic is *There Is a Time*. Growing up in the church my whole life, I have heard this scripture from Ecclesiastes 3:1-8 time and time again. Yet, it wasn't until I saw the words put into motion that I was truly touched by its message. Seeing everyone's interpretation of this scripture made me break away from my personal interpretation of the text and see the scripture in a new light. Some of the lines and phrases from this scripture I never completely understood until now. Other lines and phrases I only had a very shallow understanding of until today's sharing of the dances."

CHAPTER 3

Intention in Liturgical Dance

How is liturgical dance different from dancing in a dance recital or other secular venues? Can any dance style or genre be used as a form of dance in worship? These questions will be addressed within this chapter, but first let me begin with the basic areas of intention for liturgical dance. Prior to using liturgical dance in worship, preparation needs to occur on the part of the host church or worship community and the choreographer or director of the participating liturgical dancers. Questions need to be asked and addressed prior to embarking on this journey to use liturgical dance within liturgy or within other contexts.

People are used to seeing dance in concert, film, television, internet, and other venues. Worship communities, for the most part, are comfortable using the spoken or sung word and occasional guest artists of various types within worship. However, there are still many people who are not used to seeing the art of dance within worship.

As a teacher, performer, and choreographer in both secular and sacred dance, I have learned volumes about intention. From chapter 1, I have mentioned that *secular dance* is "any type of dance not associated with sacred, religious, or spiritual matters,"[1] and *sacred* and *liturgical dance* are types of dance "set apart and

---

1. Jewell, *Oxford American Desk Dictionary and Thesaurus*, 754.

PART I—Liturgical Dance: A Background

intended for the worship of a god."[2] There *is* a difference between what a liturgical dancer does in sharing dance in worship, and what a secular dancer does in performing in a concert or recital outside of worship. The main difference is the intention of what, where, and how the dance is used.

Dance used within worship may occur in a variety of genres such as ballet, modern, jazz, contemporary, tap, hip-hop, folk, ethnic, interpretive, and sometimes signing movements. It does not matter what the style of dance used for liturgical dance is, as long as the intention is one of worship. In order for the most positive outcome to occur, it is important that the liturgical dancer know the type of worshipping community and their preferred manner of worship prior to sharing dance in worship.

Three Areas of Intention in Liturgical Dance

1. Liturgical dance is intended as a dance of worship for God.
2. Liturgical dance offers those present a clear visual enhancement intended to lead the worshipping community into a deeper connection with God.
3. Liturgical dance allows the dancer who is sharing within worship an artistic and physical means of worshipping God.

1. *Liturgical dance is intended as a dance of worship for God.* When a dancer performs a dance, she may be doing so for any number of reasons: self-expression, communication through movement, the sheer joy of dancing, exercise, display of dance technique, or part of belonging to something greater than the self. When a dancer is sharing a *liturgical dance* within worship, the dancer must clarify the intention of her dance as one of worship for God. The intention is not entertainment, although at times a liturgical dance may be entertaining. However, entertainment is not the goal or intention of liturgical dance.

---

2. Ibid., 735.

Intention in Liturgical Dance

With the practice of liturgical dance in worship comes an important role of responsibility to the witnessing worshippers. The liturgical dancer of choreographed or sometimes improvised liturgical dance is performing visible worship, enabling those present a clearer communion with the Holy as she brings the spoken or sung words to life through movement. Therefore, the dancer is a visual aid for the worshippers while she is dancing for God. Those sharing liturgical dance within worship, whether in solo or group dances, must be keenly aware of this responsibility. Liturgical dancers should never leave the worshipping community wondering about what they are viewing through vague, confusing, or overused movements within their dance of worship.

As a teacher of dance majors at the university level, I have seen many gifted and technically trained dancers who are amazing performers. In Moving Liturgy Dance Ensemble, my liturgical dance troupe, the dancers are technically trained, but also have a heart and faith basis for liturgical dance. Ronald Gagne states, "It is important to keep in mind that there are special qualities necessary if dance is to be used in the liturgy. It must be prayerful and faith-filled. Also, it must not be simply 'professional,' the transfer of secular dance to religious surroundings."[3]

On some occasions I have seen professional dancers perform liturgical dance with flawless technique and perfect focus. Their dance ability was stunning. Often the technical ability may be enough, but at times the dancers left me void of feeling and disconnected to the liturgy. This was often due to a lack of spiritual presence and lack of understanding or connection to the content about which they were dancing. Sometimes dances look like they have been taken right out of last year's spring dance recital or dance competition and placed in the church sanctuary. Thoughtful consideration needs to be given to what is appropriate in particular settings with intent and purpose within the liturgy, not just because the dancer is a member of the church and *can dance*.

Children's liturgical dance groups, when performed with naiveté, but also with spiritual focus and authenticity, can be quite

---

3. Gagne, "The Place of Movement in the Liturgical Dance of Today," 70.

PART I—Liturgical Dance: A Background

moving. I have had the opportunity to witness many children's liturgical dance groups at a variety of levels. Some of their dances shared in worship were enhancing of the liturgy, while others were sometimes a distraction. Even well-intentioned children's groups can sometimes cause a distraction in worship if not properly supervised and may even cause some worshippers to go into what I call "recital mode," cheering for their little ones and getting out a camera in the service. By this time, the liturgical dance has slipped into the entertainment realm and it may be difficult to find one's place back into worship. It is always a matter of intention as to how it is handled and where it is placed within the worship liturgy. When used as a supporting catalyst for worship, even young dancers need to know the difference and demeanor between secular dance and worship dance while their movements and focus are kept simple, clear, and within their capabilities.

On one occasion, I was privileged to be invited to a Catholic conference where I taught a men's group an abstract liturgical dance. At the completion of the workshop, when the men shared their final dance, I was in tears, touched to my very core. Although these men had never had a dance class prior to this experience, their liturgical dance offerings were emotionally, physically, and spiritually moving. These men felt free enough to share their collective and individual dances of worship with clear intention with all present. It was one of the most compelling and intense experiences I have ever witnessed as dance in worship. Whether experienced or inexperienced in any setting, it is paramount to establish a safe and trusting environment where dancers feel comfortable and empowered to share their movements in an open and personal manner before others.

Intention in Liturgical Dance

Asking, Ingrid Murphy, Betsy Reeves, and Anita Davis, photo by Jane Wellford.

2. Liturgical dance should offer those present a clear visual enhancement intended to lead the worshipping community into a deeper connection with God. Sometimes well-intentioned dancers within worship tend to perform over-simplified and repetitive gestures in liturgical dances that are unclear or vague. If the dance

PART I—Liturgical Dance: A Background

performed does not clarify or enhance the liturgy, it may cause the witnessing worshippers to struggle with its intention. Dancers performing liturgical dance should at least try to be clear and focused so that communication transfers what is intended and worship is enhanced. Over-used or vague movements used by dancers in worship are just like a poorly written essay or an overcooked casserole—full of boring words or a bland taste!

After teaching numerous workshops on placement and body posturing for liturgical dance, I created a term I call *communal presence*. The term refers to the upper half of the dancer's body, where most of the communication occurs from dancer to worshipping community. I chose the term *communal presence* from the word "commune," which means "to speak confidently and intimately, to feel in close touch with."[4] The physical area of the dancer's body I reference with this term is the head, neck, shoulders, and upper torso of the dancer, especially the focus of the face and eyes. The body must be void of any tension or self-affectations for this open and welcoming posture to occur with clarity of focus and confident presence. This is suggested posturing for the liturgical dancer, particularly when sharing such dances as processionals in the aisles and in the transept when closest to the congregation. *Communal presence* is an invitational, confident, and welcoming presence.

The word *communal* further means "relating to or benefiting a community."[5] I view the liturgical dancer as a type of *conduit*, one who channels or reflects the message, the spirit, the words, and the music, all in one interpretive dancing body, to those present in worship. The dancer's facial expression in the *communal presence* must clearly express what is going on within the dance, or the connection from dancer to those worshipping will not be made. When a competent liturgical or sacred dancer with clear focus shares dance with worshippers, then there is charismatic potential to inspire and be a witness beyond where the words alone take the viewer. To the contrary, when the *communal presence* of the dancer

4. Jewell, *Oxford American Desk Dictionary and Thesaurus*, 151
5. Ibid., 151.

Intention in Liturgical Dance

is disconnected from what is being communicated, and the arms are limp or half-hearted, and the posture of the dancer is deficient, then the intended message through the dancer may not be communicated to those worshipping. This *communal presence* posture and body placement has options for shift in energy and focus if the choreography calls for a dramatic character or role change for the dancer. For much of liturgical dance, however, this *communal presence* of posture holds true.

Some liturgical dancers are professional, while others are not. Although being a professional is certainly not a prerequisite for being a liturgical dancer, being prepared and educationally informed for this participatory experience is important. It is a good idea for the dancer to know and understand the church liturgy and the order of worship of the church in which the dancer is sharing. Often within choreographed liturgical dances, there are times when all dancers are required to move in unison. It is the responsibility of the liturgical dance director to assist the dancers with movement and focus that is clear and unified for optimal meaning and intention. Whether the dancers are young or old, beginning or experienced, the director of the group should not send any dancers into the worship space to share a choreographed dance unless the dancers are rehearsed and focused. If it is a badly shared liturgical dance, then it will turn off the worshipping community to future opportunities for liturgical dance in worship.

There are also un-choreographed, free-form spontaneous liturgical dances that may occur within worship during any part of the worship liturgy. These dances may be found within worship communities where spontaneous dance is welcomed within liturgy. Sometimes during a hymn or anthem, or within a prayer, people feel free to dance, twirl, or sway when the spirit moves them within the music, the spoken words, or in the silence. Depending on the worshipping community, this is certainly a valid way of sharing or experiencing liturgical dance and sacred dance.

Much like the sermon is the word of God through speech and the songs sung by the choir are the word of God through song, liturgical dance is the embodiment of the word through movement.

PART I—Liturgical Dance: A Background

Whether performed by beginners who are often quite gifted, or by professionals who occasionally fall short, the dancer assumes important responsibility as one of those leading in worship like a member of the choir, a lay reader, or other worship leaders.

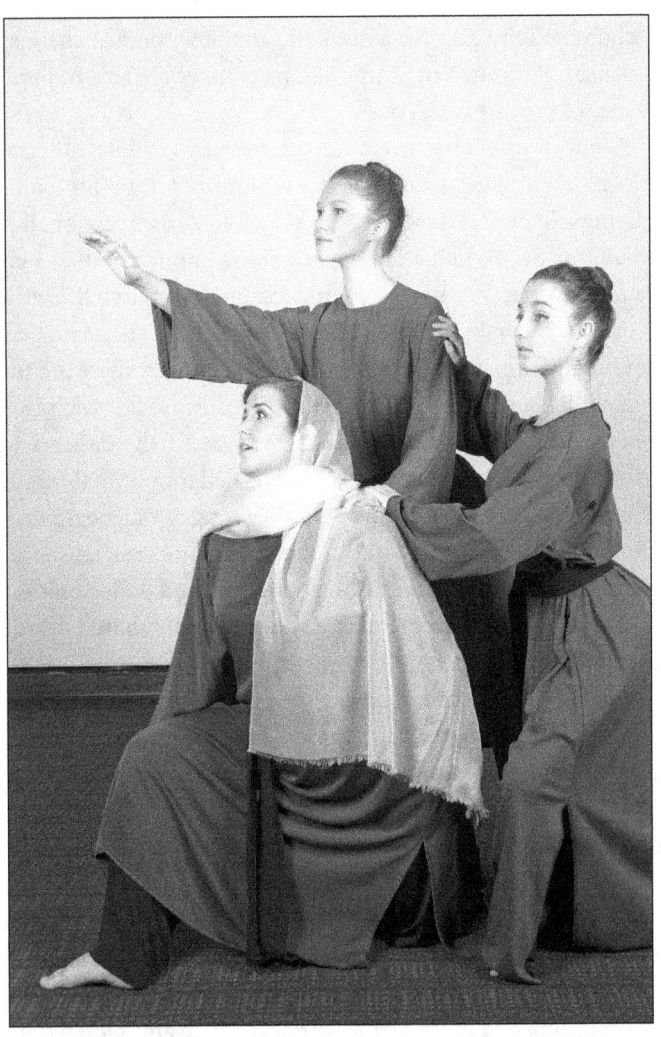

Three Marys, Heather Zachary, Fiona Koch, and Leigh Stanfill, photo by Kim Walker.

Intention in Liturgical Dance

Steve Rooks, former principal dancer with the Martha Graham Dance Company, states the following with regard to Christian dance.

> There's been a tendency sometimes to think that Christian Art is a watered down version of good art and that's just not the case at all. A lot of artists who have a firm faith in Christ are rising to the challenge and they are doing their arts in excellence. There is a level of personal integrity and I think the world is going to see something quite different.[6]

In addition to being well rehearsed, another area of preparation for the liturgical dancer is a knowledge and understanding in religious education with at least a general on-going study of *The Bible*. Since Christian liturgical dance is based on Christian scriptures and supporting texts from scholarly Christian theologians, it is important that the dancer is knowledgeable in this faith. A good choreographer or director of liturgical dance will enhance this knowledge through choreography that has both an informed and theological understanding of scripture and supporting texts within the dance. Both analysis and reflective study need to take place when interpreting scripture and songs of Christian content for liturgical dance. When the liturgical dancer has an informed background in the faith, in addition to knowledge and understanding of music where music is used, the integrity of the shared dance and ownership of the movements are greatly enhanced.

3. Liturgical dance allows the dancer sharing within worship an artistic and physical means of worshipping God. This third and final intention of liturgical dance allows the liturgical dancer a *personal* artistic and physical means of worshipping God through dance. A prepared dancer who has rehearsed her dance is able to present and *live in* the movements as she shares the embodiment of her worship to God. She is fully dancing her worship as she shares her danced prayer or other liturgical dance offering. Although the

---

6. Rooks, *Project Dance Foundation*, Internet website, 2010, http://projectdance.com?page_id=181

PART I—Liturgical Dance: A Background

experience of dancing in worship allows the dancer an important personal worship experience, since the dance is shared in the presence of others, it carries the same responsibilities mentioned earlier in this chapter regarding intention and leadership responsibility.

— PART II —

Laying the Foundation for Liturgical Dance

CHAPTER 4

The Host Church or Worship Community

WHEN CONSIDERING USING LITURGICAL dance within one's church or worship community, many churches begin through discussions with a worship committee. This committee might be composed of clergy or other worship leaders together with volunteer members from the congregation. A worship committee meets on a regular basis for the purpose of determining the structure and content of the worship services. The host worship committee may want to consider the following questions when using liturgical dance.

10 Important Questions Regarding the Use of Liturgical Dance

1. What is liturgical dance? Does our church fully understand the definition, history, and background of dance in liturgy?

2. How do we go about searching for information regarding liturgical dance? Where do we find a liturgical dance specialist who can answer our questions regarding our church's interest in this worship art?

3. How do we educate our church regarding liturgical dance?

PART II—Laying the Foundation for Liturgical Dance

4. Who may perform liturgical dance in worship? Can anyone do this?
5. We may have dancers and/or choreographers in our church. Should we ask them to perform liturgical dance in our worship, or bring in a professional troupe?
6. Once we have decided to have liturgical dance in our worship, who will act as liaison between the liturgical dancers and our church to ensure this experience runs smoothly for our church and the dancers?
7. Where would we like the liturgical dance to occur? This pertains to where within the *order of worship* itself as well as where within the particular *physical space*?
8. Have we ever had liturgical dance within our church's history? Was it a positive or a negative experience? How was it received? Make sure this is not one person's opinion, but rather a collective answer given by worship leaders and congregation members who experienced the same event.
9. Why do we specifically want liturgical dance in our worship? Are we searching for a new means of worship that will enhance what we already have in place?
10. Is this something both the worship leaders and the congregation would like to occur within worship?

It is a good idea to begin with questions such as 1-10 since each church's interest and needs are unique. Answers to Questions 1-7 will be answered in this chapter. Questions 8-10 must be answered by the individual host church or worship community.

The Host Church or Worship Community

Celebration, Anita Davis, Ginger Strickland, Jane Wellford, Betsy Reeves, Ingrid Murphy, photo by Debbie Lynch.

1. What is liturgical dance? The answer to this question is provided in chapter 1 and in *Glossary A* of this text. Other authorities on the subject may be found online under such subject areas as *liturgical dance* and *sacred dance* or through *The Sacred Dance Guild,* an international organization with an accessible website. Additional locations may be in books, scholarly journals, encyclopedias, seminaries, university religious studies departments, and in churches that have existing worship arts. The following examples are where dance is noted within scriptures of *The Bible,* through actual accounts or through metaphoric reference.

Exodus 15:20

Exodus 32:19

Judges 11:34

Judges 21:21

I Samuel 18:6

I Samuel 21:11

I Samuel 30:16

II Samuel 6:14

PART II—Laying the Foundation for Liturgical Dance

Psalms 30:11

Psalms 149:3

Psalms 150:4

Ecclesiastes 3:4

Jeremiah 31:4

Lamentations 5:15

Matthew 11:17

Luke 15:25

2. How do we go about searching for information regarding liturgical dance? Where do we find a liturgical dance specialist who can answer specific questions regarding our church's interest in usage of this artistic worship ministry? The following are places/locations to begin your search:

Internet—Search topic areas as: Liturgical Dance, Sacred Dance, Dance in Worship, Arts in Worship, and Dance History

Libraries—Books, journals, and other periodicals on sacred or liturgical dance

Sacred Dance Guild International, online at http://sacreddanceguild.org/

Seminaries with arts in worship programs and courses

Churches with arts in worship programs

Local Colleges and Universities: Dance Departments, Performing Arts Departments, Religious Studies Departments

Arts Councils and Arts Guilds: local, state, and national

Church Administrative Councils, Synods, or other church governing bodies

Dance Studios and listings for liturgical dance classes and liturgical dance troupes

3. How do we educate our church regarding liturgical dance?

Guest speaker—Invite a liturgical dance specialist guest speaker, or have them as one of several speakers as part of an *Arts in Worship* series for your church.

The Host Church or Worship Community

Workshops—Invite a liturgical dance specialist to lead a workshop on liturgical dance for your church that is open to all, for worship leaders and members of the worship committee, for the youth, for the community, or for a church collective experience.

Professional dance troupe—Invite a liturgical dance troupe to perform a dance of worship within your existing worship, always including some educational information regarding liturgical dance in your bulletin to educate the congregation about what they will be experiencing.

Flyers and educational information—Provide flyers with liturgical dance information to place in church foyers, classrooms, bulletin boards, church newsletters, and bulletin inserts.

Sunday school discussions—Assign "what is liturgical dance" as a class question within a Sunday school class when studying forms of worship.

Pentecost, Anita Davis, Ginger Strickland, Betsy Reeves, and Ingrid Murphy, photo by Bethany Cubino.

4. Who may perform liturgical dance in worship? Can anyone do this? Anyone may perform liturgical dance in worship. It is also important to know, understand, and respect the intention of this worship art. (*See Chapter 3: Intention in Liturgical Dance*) Whether a church decides to use beginning, intermediate, advanced or

PART II—Laying the Foundation for Liturgical Dance

professional dancers, understanding intention is important. Liturgical dance is a form of dance set apart from secular dance. It must be handled with care when used within worship by anyone wishing to incorporate it, with oversight by an individual experienced in this worship art.

Dance in worship is not reserved only for the youth of a church, either in the doing or the receiving of liturgical dance. All ages, sexes, and abilities may participate in this worship art and are encouraged to do so. I had the opportunity to choreograph an Advent cantata for a church where I used thirty-five members of the congregation, ages four to eighty-two! Even today, this large church says that the experience of so many of their members participating within worship in such an artistic collaborative experience was one of the highlights of their church's history.

5. We may have dancers and/or choreographers in our church. Should we ask them to perform liturgical dance in our worship, or bring in a professional troupe? Many times, congregations will want to use dancers and/or choreographers who are members of their church to dance in worship. Wonderful! However, be careful not to assume that because dancers *can dance*, they can do *liturgical dance* (see Chapter 6: *Preparation for the Liturgical Dancer*). Remember that *secular dance* and *liturgical dance* have two different purposes. The director of the liturgical dancers should assist those dancing in worship to be mindful of intention rather than allowing any possible self-promoting within the worship opportunity (see Chapter 5: *The Director or Choreographer of Liturgical Dance*).

It takes understanding or knowledge of the content being portrayed through the dance as well as some degree of dance or movement ability to share liturgical dance within worship. This ability may be taught to anyone within the congregation by a gifted director of liturgical dance. The content may be simplistic or advanced, and it may take a little time and training to develop, but anyone can learn with training and rehearsal. The choreographer and/or dance director should rehearse the dancers prior to having dancers share in worship. If a congregation has dancers within its

The Host Church or Worship Community

membership, this is a great first step. Clear focus of the face, articulate movements, and awareness of the dancer's *communal presence* (see *Chapter 3: Intention in Liturgical Dance*) are areas that need to be most clearly taught for liturgical dancers to be effective within worship.

6. Once we have decided to have liturgical dance in our worship, who will act as liaison between the liturgical dancers and our church to ensure this experience runs smoothly? It is important to have a main contact person, or *liaison*, between the internal or external group of dancers. This individual will take care of all communication between the host church and the dancers. The role of the liaison might include the following:

Photos of the Space—Since knowledge of the space is very important for the choreographer and dancers to know about ahead of time, the liaison should share photos of the space where the dance will occur with the choreographer and dancers in advance. It is necessary for the choreographer to have spatial measurements as well as a photo of the space prior to creating any dance for worship, especially if the dancers are from outside the church, coming from a distance away. Photos of the space may be sent to the choreographer by e-mail, fax, or traditional mail several weeks or months in advance. If there is a need to move any church furnishings, always ask for permission first from the church. Some items are easily movable and others are not. The dancers need to be made aware of what space will be available for the dance to occur, and whether or not platforms or other items may need to be brought in for greater visibility of the dance

Rehearsals—Set up pre-event spacing and music rehearsals with those working in collaboration with dancers such as musicians, singers, readers, technicians, custodians or others involved in the planning of the worship service. It is important to send a recorded copy of the music and the sheet music to the choreographer in advance to make sure of the correct musical arrangement and appropriate timing.

PART II—Laying the Foundation for Liturgical Dance

Technical Needs—Set up any required technical needs: microphones, podiums, and amplifiers for musicians, singers, readers, and/or pre-recorded music needs if pre-recorded music is allowed in the particular church.

Fees—If a fee is charged by an outside liturgical dance troupe, request a check from the church treasurer. If possible, request to have the check ready for the guest group on the day of the event.

Publicity and Education—Promote education and publicity ahead of time if this is to be a successful experience. Bulletin inserts, an article in the church newsletter, flyers on church bulletin boards, and oral announcements are helpful. Within the community, contact the newspaper, radio, television stations, local dance studios, college/university dance and religious studies departments, local churches, and seminaries and social media websites.

Advocate—Act as a guardian or advocate for the liturgical dancers regarding the dancer's space in case other members of the church may not be aware of changes for this specific service. There may be a change in placement of physical items within the service such as portable communion rails, communion table, podiums, pulpit, flower stands, music stands, microphones, or bell choir tables. The liaison is in charge of making sure the dancers' space is maintained before and throughout the worship service(s). Here is one example of a problem my liturgical dance troupe encountered. An uninformed congregational member placed unexpected objects in the path of the dancers minutes before the service began. Such objects causing sabotage included spontaneously placed music stands, pennies for hunger baskets in the aisles, and a lit advent wreath! These types of incidents could potentially cause accidents or injury to the dancers in worship on any given Sunday, but could most certainly wreck a liturgical dance shared within worship.

7. Where and when would the church like the liturgical dance to occur? This pertains to where within the order of worship, and where within the particular physical space of worship.

Once the church has made the decision to have liturgical dance within its worship, the church must decide on the location.

The Host Church or Worship Community

Many churches prefer to have liturgical dance woven into the existing liturgy of the worship service in the main sanctuary. Some elect to have liturgical dance in the fellowship hall or other alternative space. Wherever the location, please allow the dancers as much space as possible to share their liturgical dance. Remember that liturgical dance is the *visual* sharing of the word of God through movement, often in collaboration with the spoken or sung word. It must be visible for clear communication and message transfer to occur. If certain church furnishings need to be moved with permission of the host church, they can be moved right back into place after the service, and often within the service (communion table, communion rails, music stands, or baptismal fonts).

It is also important for the liturgical dance to be placed within the appropriate place within the *order of worship*. It should have an intentional purpose for being within the service just like the sermon, the hymns, and the prayers. Common places liturgical dance might be used within the order of worship are: Call to worship, scripture readings, hymn processionals and recessionals, prayers, anthems, litanies, children's messages, and sometimes used as the main sermon.

Questions 8–10 will need to be answered by the worship committee or worship community itself. The key to success in any new worship endeavor for the church or worship community is education. Once the church has decided to use liturgical dance within worship, the worship committee must inform and educate the church about what the church will be experiencing *before* the event takes place for the most successful outcome.

CHAPTER 5

The Director or Choreographer of Liturgical Dance

THE DIRECTOR OR CHOREOGRAPHER of liturgical dance should be knowledgeable and/or proficient in two main areas: dance and the faith which the choreographer/director is creating her worship art to reflect. A gifted liturgical dance director or choreographer can work with anyone, trained or untrained, to bring this worship art to fruition. It would be wonderful for the liturgical dance director to have a background in any or all of the following areas: (1) dance, (2) choreography, (3) knowledge of the faith to which the dance pertains, (4) rehearsal direction, and (5) public relations experience.

Numerous dance genres, or styles of dance, are available as possibilities to praise and worship God. Who is to say that one style is more suited for worship than another? From modern, ballet, contemporary, hip-hop, jazz, ethnic, folk, tap, musical theatre, signing, or any combination of these, dances of worship may be created. The choreographer's dances may reflect joy, celebration, thanksgiving, humor, brokenness, reflection, repentance, and questions. Liturgical dance may be contemporary or classical, narrative or abstract. The only limits are the choreographer's vision and the appropriate match with the worshipping community. Because this is a delicate balance of religion and the arts, it is important that these dances are clear in intention and well-rehearsed before putting them before a worshipping community.

The Director or Choreographer of Liturgical Dance

Handle the creative process and rehearsals from the very beginning with care, being mindful of potential "land mines" or "sacred cows" within the worshipping community. As one of the dancers in *Moving Liturgy Dance Ensemble* often reminds me, "Don't give those worshipping a bullet to use in their gun to shoot you down."[1] You are up front and center in *their* worship, which is a boat some might be afraid to rock. Just enter this arena with educational preparation, respect, and informed intention. Dance can be very direct, powerful, and prophetic at times and cause the worshippers to see the word in a fresh new way. It is up to the choreographer to reveal how beautiful, arresting, and inspirational this form of worship can be for everyone involved.

Recommendations for the Liturgical Dance Director or Choreographer

1. Knowledge of liturgical dance and all that this implies, knowing the differences between liturgical dance and secular dance.

2. Knowledge and/or experience of the craft of choreography and how this applies to analysis and study of the religious material that is to be communicated.

3. Knowledge and understanding of religious education in the Christian faith that is communicated through the choreography and intention of the dance.

4. Knowledge of church liturgy, rubrics, and style of worship of the particular congregation with which you are participating in worship.

5. Past history of any liturgical dance in the church you will be sharing prior to the sharing of your liturgical dance with this particular church.

---

1. Reeves, Associate Director of Moving Liturgy Dance Ensemble, Interview, 2014.

PART II—Laying the Foundation for Liturgical Dance

Peace, Jane Wellford, photo by Jack Sink.

6. Awareness and respect of the collaborative nature of working with church clergy, musicians, and other church personnel.
7. Foundational knowledge of music and theatre are assets to this position, especially regarding musical choices and presentational style of dances.

8. Awareness of spatial differences and restrictions in church sanctuaries as opposed to secular stages or other dance venues.

Questions for the Liturgical Dance Director to Ask the Host Church or Worship Community

The director of the liturgical dancers should have an initial meeting with the host church liaison or worship committee who has extended the invitation. It is important to have this meeting well in advance of the worship event. This may be in person, e-mail, skype, or by phone. At this initial meeting, the liturgical dance director might ask the following questions:

1. Is your church familiar with liturgical dance?

2. Has your church ever experienced liturgical dance within worship before? If so, was it well received by the worshipping community, or was it a negative experience?

3. If using liturgical dance is a "repeat experience" for your church, how would your church wish to envision this next experience of liturgical dance within worship?

4. Would your church like liturgical dance woven into your existing worship service, or would you like a concert of dances of worship separate from your worship service?

5. If used within your worship service, where in the order of service would you like the dances to occur? Possible placements might include the following: as an opening processional dance, during the call to worship, as a prayer, offertory anthem, hymn, benediction, recessional hymn, children's message, or within a cantata.

6. In what physical space will the liturgical dance occur: sanctuary, fellowship hall, or other location? What is the space like? Ask for photos and spatial dimensions to be sent by internet, fax, or traditional mail. If you notice sight line problems from photos or an on-site visit, ask if certain objects are able to

PART II—Laying the Foundation for Liturgical Dance

be moved. Some church furnishings are portable and easily moved. Potential spatial problems within the worship space might include a pulpit, communion table, lectern, baptismal font, bell choir tables, or other church furnishings. Do not expect these things will automatically be moved. Remember that worship in many churches most often occurs with speaking and singing, not movement. Church personnel are sometimes not used to making these spatial allowances. Therefore, you must ask because you are a guest in their space. Spatial accommodations may often be made.

7. How much time do I have to prepare—two weeks, four weeks, or six months?

8. In addition to dance within your worship service, would you like a liturgical dance workshop for any interest groups within your church?

9. What is your congregation like—progressive, conservative, or other?

10. What type of music does your worship community feel comfortable using in worship—classical, contemporary, gospel, ethnic, world, or a mix?

11. Does your church have a policy regarding the use of prerecorded music in worship? Is there a possibility of using prerecorded music for some of the liturgical dances, or would your worship committee prefer all the music for the liturgical dance to be live? If the latter, the choreographer will need to contact the church's director of music to discuss musical accompaniment that is agreeable with both the liturgical dance director and the worship community. A copy of the sheet music and a rehearsal recording should be provided for the liturgical dance director as soon as live music is requested for successful collaboration of dance with live music. For further information, see chapter 8 in the section *Dancers Working with Musicians*.

The Director or Choreographer of Liturgical Dance

Forgive Us Our Trespasses, Matthew Baker, Sam Eisenstadt, Miles Williams, photo by Kim Walker.

12. May the dancers come to the church for a spacing rehearsal prior to sharing on the actual worship event date? If working in collaboration with musicians or readers, arrange for a joint rehearsal *following* the dancers' spacing rehearsal. The dancers' spacing rehearsal and the joint collaborative rehearsal with musicians or readers may occur any time prior to the

PART II—Laying the Foundation for Liturgical Dance

event, but it is imperative that both occur for the worship service to proceed smoothly.

13. Is someone available for set-up and technical support prior to and/or during the event? If pre-recorded music is used, there will need to be a sound technician available.

Choreographic Suggestions and Other Important Information for the Liturgical Dance Choreographer

The choreographer of liturgical dance is entrusted with the major responsibility of creating movements for the dancer that will enable the worshipping community to experience a more multi-dimensional worship service. Helpful tried and true tips for choreography in liturgical dance include the following:

1. Choreograph according to both the age as well as the ability of the liturgical dancers. Challenge advanced dancers, and keep choreography simple and clear for beginning dancers.

2. Think of your choreographed dance as a well-written paper and ask these questions:

    a. Are you using movements that are perhaps too simple or too similar to reveal a clear and understandable story for the viewers?

    b. Are your dance movements too technical, too abstract, or too bizarre for viewers to understand?

    c. Are the transitions between movement phrasings smooth and well-connected?

    d. Are you using a variety of spatial levels in your movement choices (high, middle, and low) in your choreography? Dances that use the same level of movement throughout the dance tend to be "vanilla" and boring. Varied levels of movement as well as changes in energy dynamics create a more interesting dance.

The Director or Choreographer of Liturgical Dance

3. Communication is the point of liturgical dance through your artistry. Choose movements that are clear and easily understood. At the same time, try not to insult or over-simplify for the viewer. These movements should arrest the viewer's attention and enhance communication for those worshipping. Perhaps choose a tasteful mixture of literal and abstract movements within a song or text. It is a good idea to ask for a "second eye" or another person's opinion in the early stages of creation or rehearsals long before completion of the dance. Perhaps go out into the nave or seating area of the sanctuary and take a look at your choreography from a worshipper's perspective before your dance is ready to share in worship.

4. Awareness of sightline constraints within the sanctuary is important. Remember, most seated worshippers can only see a liturgical dancer from the waist up unless the dancer is dancing in a raised chancel area, on a platform, or on a stage space within the sanctuary. Often your choreography has to be re-worked when you are surprised by your worship space and have not done an on-site visit or viewed photographs of the space prior to the event. Many older sanctuaries are flat, or have almost no space for dancing up front. The choreographer may have a great deal of re-choreographing to do once in a new space, working around communion rails, baptismal fonts, lecterns, pulpits, steps, music stands, etc. Many low-level movements within choreography may need to be changed to medium-level or high-level movements within the dance due to sightline constraints.

PART II—Laying the Foundation for Liturgical Dance

Awakened by Grace, Leah Palmer, Sarah Beacham,
photo by Randy Piland.

5. Spacing rehearsal is a must for dancers! Have a spacing rehearsal in the worship space with your dancers *only* first. After you have worked out any spacing issues within the new environment, you may then have additional rehearsals with the musicians and readers. When working with musicians and readers, you will often have to stop and start due

The Director or Choreographer of Liturgical Dance

to timing issues of music or reading with dance. But a *dance spacing rehearsal* is not necessary for musicians, singers, and readers to sit through prior to their final run-through with the dancers before the worship event.

6. When choreographing dance for an opening processional in worship where flags or banners are carried by dancers, consider asking ahead of time that perhaps an announcement is printed in the bulletin for the congregation to remain seated as they sing the opening hymn. This is not always necessary but may be important for safety as well as visibility reasons for the congregation in case dancers may be carrying flags or banners as they process. At times, a congregation member has been caressed in the face by over-zealous flag waving dancers entering down the aisles. The congregation standing and singing while dancers enter down the aisles is usually a non-issue if dancers are not carrying anything large when entering down the aisles.

7. Assist the dancers in understanding the difference between liturgical dance and being in a dance recital. Do your dancers understand they are participating as a visual enhancement within the worship service, much like the members of the choir when they sing their anthems? Do they understand that they are to stay and participate as guest worshippers within the service and not bow and leave like in a dance recital? Since I have opened the "etiquette" door, let me continue. Does the minister bow after sharing the sermon? Does the choir bow and expect applause after their singing? If you answered "no" to these questions, then as participants within the worship service like the minister and the choir, the liturgical dancers are not entertainers and should most often quietly return to their seats after their shared dance within worship. There are varied responses in churches regarding protocol after different components of worship are shared. Each church may find its own way as to whether to sit in silence, or to respond with "Amen" or applause. It often

PART II—Laying the Foundation for Liturgical Dance

has to do with what is being shared within worship, whether it is meant to be responded to with introspective silence and meditation, or met with shouts of joy.

CHAPTER 6

Preparation for the Liturgical Dancer

THE LITURGICAL DANCER MAY already be a gifted dancer, well-trained in one form of dance or another. On the other hand, the individual sharing liturgical dance may have no dance training at all. It is recommended that first time liturgical dancers have some assistance and direction from an experienced individual in dance as well as an understanding of the faith in which they are sharing their artistry. Anyone may participate in liturgical dance, but beginners need guidance as to *when* to dance in worship, *what movements* they might use, and knowledge of the *difference between dance in worship* and *secular dance*. It's all about intention as well as thoughtful preparation for the experience.

The dancer should request information about the congregation or worshipping community with whom the dancer is sharing liturgical dance. Does this church know anything about liturgical dance? Is the liturgical dance presentation being shared the church's first encounter with this worship art? If the answer is the latter question, enter this arena with education, information, and respect for the unknown. If this is a first endeavor for this congregation, make sure the dance is well rehearsed and thoughtfully crafted, especially if used within the liturgy. Some congregations may have problems when it comes to dance used in worship.

PART II—Laying the Foundation for Liturgical Dance

The physical body is at times a stumbling block for certain individuals, whether used as a worship aid or in life in general. When dance is used within worship before a worshipping community, the dancer must be mindful not to make her dance a private experience and exclude the worshippers who are viewing. This could easily become a distraction for those present and cause confusion within the worship as to the intention of the dance. There is usually intention on the liturgical dancer's part to communicate the word of God to everyone present in worship, acting as a channel or conduit to enable others to hear *and see* the words through movement. When a liturgical dance is externalized, it becomes a corporate experience and a message of visual communication.

Preparation for liturgical dance begins long before the dancer enters the sanctuary. Being ever mindful of her responsibility, the dancer is aware that she is dancing for God *and* the worshipping community. This enables a more multi-sensory worship experience for the community while providing the dancer's own opportunity for spiritual worship. The dancer or dancers may either be volunteers from within the church, or professional dancers invited from outside the church.

Prior to Dancing in Worship, It is Suggested That The Liturgical Dancer is Mindful of the Following

1. *Spend time in prayer* prior to the service, reflecting on what you as a dancer are to do: dance for God and the worshipping community.

2. *Be warmed up* physically and prepared to share the liturgical dance. The dancer's body and mind need to be in the right place. It is important to have at least a thirty minute stretch and flexibility warm-up prior to sharing the dance of worship. Know the dance ahead of time so that concern and worry are not present. The dancer should know the dance well enough to *live in* the movements that are expressed through the dancer's body and focus. There is nothing quite so ineffective

as seeing a dancer struggling through the steps, saying the counts aloud, trying to copy others in the dance, or allowing her focus to stray as those in worship are trying their best to receive the message of the dance. This can easily occur from time to time with young or novice liturgical dancers of any age. The liturgical dance director should rehearse the dancers well, encouraging them every step of the way to avoid any poor preparation issues.

Assurance of Pardon, Fiona Koch, Leigh Stanfill, photo by Kim Walker.

3. *Maintain an attitude of reverence and respect within the service,* both when dancing and not dancing. From the time the dancer enters the sanctuary, the liturgical dancer's presence is noticed by others. The dancer is often wearing some sort of costume while sitting within the sanctuary. Therefore the dancer's presence is obvious. The liturgical dancer is one of the leaders within worship like a member of the choir, or a reader assisting in worship. The liturgical dancer must be mindful of this when participating in worship, awaiting her time to dance. Since the congregation notices even small differences and changes within the worship, the liturgical dancer should maintain a respectful presence during worship.

PART II—Laying the Foundation for Liturgical Dance

4. *Focus is everything!* This is the most important area of communication for the liturgical dance to be successful. The dancer must be clearly and energetically focused when sharing the movements of the dance. It is not just a state of mind focus for the dancer, but a physical placement of where the dancer is looking with energy, intent, and emotional integrity. If the dancer doesn't *believe* the dance, neither will the congregation. For example, if a choreographer has called for a dancer to reach upward and look up to where the hand is reaching, and the dancer's focus is not where the hand is reaching but off to the side or on the floor somewhere, then the intention to be conveyed is lost or misunderstood. Much more rehearsal needs to occur for the dancer to ensure her focus and intention are clear in the dance. *Chapter 3: Intention in Litugical Dance* regarding communal presence addresses this further.

5. *Rehearse in the actual worship space* where the dance will occur prior to the worship service. Sanctuary spaces and stage spaces are quite different. Stage spaces are large, open rectangular areas with lots of open space, while sanctuaries commonly have multiple floor levels with steps, various obstacles of furnishings, and limited space to dance. A dance that is rehearsed in a studio space might look like one experience. But when transposed into a sanctuary setting, the dance will have a totally different look and spatial outcome of floor patterns. Before ever dancing in a sanctuary space, the dancer needs to be mindful of movable and immovable furnishings, sightline restrictions, and available floor space. Certain things such as organs and architecturally imbedded pulpits are permanent fixtures, where lecterns, music stands, baptismal fonts, bell choir tables, and pianos might more easily be moved.

6. *People as obstacles!* In addition to church furnishings, there are often people sharing leadership roles in liturgy within this same space the dancers will use. Ministers, liturgists, choir and bell choir directors, acolytes, and others must be made aware of dancers and vice versa to share the space with

Preparation for the Liturgical Dancer

respect. This will often change the intended choreography of the dancers. Variables, such as people and objects within a shared worship space, need to be known well in advance of the worship experience. This knowledge will help avoid unknown surprises and will enable the dancer to make necessary changes during the rehearsal process. Most churches are willing to allow the dancer into the worship space for spacing rehearsals prior to the event if asked in advance.

By being a prepared liturgical dancer, the outcome of the worship experience will be greatly enhanced for all involved in the collaborative experience. A liturgical dancer has the potential to share a valuable leadership role within worship when careful attention and preparation have been given to the artistic and spiritual preparations that accompany this responsibility.

Processional Entry, Betsy Reeves, photo by Kim Walker

CHAPTER 7

Where Will the Dance Occur Within the Liturgy?

WITHIN THE CATHOLIC CHURCH and the numerous denominations of the Christian faith, the structure and style of worship might look quite different depending on which house of worship one attends. When a person attends a Methodist service, she might expect one style of worship, a Baptist service, yet another style, and a Catholic service still another worship style of liturgy. Within these different Christian worship structures are various levels of formality, informality, and group dynamics. Within nondenominational Christian Churches, one might find an even wider spectrum of worship styles.

The following is an example of a worship liturgy structure from a Presbyterian Church, U.S.A. worship service. As you read the following order of worship, try to visualize times and places within the order of worship where liturgical dance might occur within this particular worship structure. I have placed an asterisk (*) and a dance suggestion where I have known and experienced dance to be very effective within this order of worship.

Order of Service

* *Prelude*—Usually instrumental music, which begins the service and may accompany an invitational liturgical dance.

Where Will the Dance Occur Within the Liturgy?

* *Call to Worship*—The worship leader, choir, or lay reader addresses the congregation as a call to focus on the worship. This may be spoken or sung words, instrumental music, or any combination of these and may include a dance. An example of a dance as a Call to Worship might be the a cappella arrangement of *Let the Words of My Mouth* by Gail Loress Hamilton from Psalm 19:14, or a dance to a reading of this text.

* *Opening hymn*—Often congregational members will stand and sing as the choir, acolyte, and possible liturgical dancers and/or other attendants enter in a processional down the aisles. It is suggested to have the dancers enter first in a processional hymn and "dance in" the first two stanzas of the hymn before the other members of the processional enter the sanctuary down the aisles into the chancel since the others, such as acolyte, choir, or clergy usually enter walking.

Call to Confession—Introduced and spoken by the minister, liturgist, or lay reader.

Prayer of Confession—A unison reading of the congregation usually led by the minister, liturgist, or lay reader.

* *Kyrie Eleison (Lord Have Mercy . . .)*—Sung by everyone present. This could be a very simple and prayerful dance shared by a soloist in the chancel area.

Assurance of Pardon—Minister or worship leader offers this pardon as the congregation listens and receives.

* *Gloria Patri (Glory be to the Father . . .)*—Sung by everyone present. This could be a joyful dance of praise and thanksgiving.

Passing of the Peace (Peace of the Lord be with you . . .)—Said to those near you with an exchange of hand clasp while making eye contact.

PART II—Laying the Foundation for Liturgical Dance

Grateful, Fiona Koch, photo by Kim Walker.

* *Children's Message*—A time for children to come to the chancel for a special message from the worship leader. I have often choreographed simple dance dramatizations of the parables of Jesus. Examples: *Sower and the Seed, The Good Samaritan, The Prodigal Son,* and many other simple teaching stories from scripture. These are great to have read, danced, and dramatized during this worship

Where Will the Dance Occur Within the Liturgy?

segment and children may be involved whenever possible. One or two rehearsals during a Sunday school class works well for this to use during church. Simple children's prayers or litanies also work well for dance interpretations during this time.

Prayer for Illumination—Liturgist or Pastor prays prior to scripture reading.

* *First Scripture Reading*—A reading from *The Holy Bible* by the worship leader or lay reader. This is one of my favorite examples of liturgical dance usage. Having the scripture reading of the day danced while a well-paced reader reads the words from the pulpit is very effective and strong as it provides a visual aid to the reading. This needs to be well-rehearsed for timing in advance with the reader.

* *Anthem*—Choir sings to musical accompaniment or a cappella. This is a great place to use liturgical dance where dancers share through movement the lyrics and music of any selected anthem.

* *Second Scripture Reading*—A reading from *The Bible* by the worship leader or lay reader. Same explanation applies as in the first scripture reading above.

* *Sermon*—Spoken message given by the worship leader from the pulpit or chancel area. On a few occasions, I have been asked to choreograph part of the sermon or share a themed dance *as* the sermon, since it is the embodiment of the word through movement. This could also be a dance drama using spoken text with dance with or without music by the dancers.

* *Affirmation of Faith*—Creed (Apostles' or Nicene) spoken in unison by everyone present. This reading can certainly be enhanced by an interpretive dance.

PART II—Laying the Foundation for Liturgical Dance

Dance of Gladness, Grace Strickland, Kennedy Bennett, and others, photo by John Moran.

Concerns of Congregation—Worship leader announces opportunity to share concerns from congregation prior to the worship leader or minister's prayer.

Minister's Prayer—Worship leader or minister prays for the church, the community, and the world.

* *Lord's Prayer*—Dance is extremely effective for this prayer. Just remind the congregation to keep their eyes open while praying or they will miss the dance they are bringing to life with their guiding words for the dancers. This could be shared to spoken words, sung words, or various musical arrangements.

Offering of Tithes and Gifts—A time for church deacons, elders, or church laity to collect offering.

* *Offertory Anthem*—This is often an anthem sung by the choir. It is a great opportunity for the congregation to sit and watch dancers bring the music and words to life through movement, and one of the most popular times for use of dance within liturgy. Any dancing should occur with the choir before or after the offering, not during.

Where Will the Dance Occur Within the Liturgy?

* *Doxology*—(*Praise God from Whom All Blessings Flow...*)—Sung by all present. A simple dance of giving thanks could be performed here on a regular basis. Or, the entire congregation could stand and do simple structured praise gestures or movements with their arms while they sing the *Doxology*.

* *Closing Hymn*—Led by choir and sung by everyone present as the congregation stands. The choir and ministers sometimes recess out of sanctuary on this final hymn. An excellent opportunity for liturgical dancers to lead the choir and ministers as they recess out during this recessional dance, symbolic of taking the spirit and congregational service out into the community at the close of worship.

* *Blessing or Benediction*—Worship leader gives a blessing and a sending forth to the congregation. Any simple benediction text or sung benediction of any type may be danced here. Example of music with vocals: *An Irish Blessing: May the Road Rise to Meet You* by Michael Patrick Murphy.

* *Postlude*—Usually instrumental music is played at the close of worship. Dance could certainly be used here, but it is often used as a time for those worshipping to sit or stand and meditate on the service prior to leaving the sanctuary.

One might imagine that dance should only be incorporated where music is played in worship and that a dancer must have music to dance. This is not always the case. Any readings of text make excellent opportunities for dance to occur and are excellent reinforcements to the spoken word. Although dance within worship may occur almost anywhere, the most common places for dance in the liturgy are the following:

    Call to Worship

    Children's Message

    Hymns

    Gloria Patri

PART II—Laying the Foundation for Liturgical Dance

Lord's Prayer or other prayers

Doxology

Litanies

Scripture Readings

Kyrie Eleison

Anthems

Affirmation of Faith or Creeds

Benediction

According to Hal Taussig in *Dancing the Scriptures*, there are specific implications for the use of dance in the church's liturgy and education. Taussig states, "Many of the texts which we are called to preach or teach were meant instead to be enacted or ritualized. A number of categories of passages encourage a dance interpretation by their own form and content."[1]

During the middle ages, the Catholic Church sanctioned four church choral dances during certain church festivals, usually carried on by the lower clergy outside of the formal church services. Although there was controversy over some dancing in the church during this time, the following four festival dances remained active during these four church festival occasions: The Priests Festival on St. John's Day, Deacon's Festival on St. Stephen's Day, sub deacons' Festival on Feast of Circumcision Day, and Choirboy's Festival on Innocent's Day.[2] Christian worship services today often have sacraments woven into their worship liturgy.

Within the Catholic Church, the following seven sacraments are practiced: Baptism, Eucharist (celebration of the Lord's Supper), Confirmation, Penance or Confession, Holy Orders (ordination), Matrimony (marriage), Unction (anointing of the sick or dead). Within protestant denominations of the Christian faith, two sacraments are practiced, Baptism and Eucharist. In addition to these two sacraments, other sacred rituals take place in the

---

1. Taussig, *Dancing the Scriptures*, 69.
2. Kraus, et al., *History of the Dance in Art and Education*, 56

Where Will the Dance Occur Within the Liturgy?

Christian church such as Confirmation, and Laying on of Hands during Ordination and Installation just to name a few.

My reason for mentioning the sacraments and other rituals within the Christian church is because liturgical dance has at times been a celebrative part of sacraments and rituals within the church throughout history. I have personally danced within the sacraments of matrimony, Eucharist, and at the rituals of ordination and installation services of clergy. Many of my sacred and liturgical dance colleagues have shared dances at these same rituals as well as at funerals. Hall Taussig states "The Bible, as the church has intuited throughout its history, has much more material that that applies directly to the worship moments of praise, confession, song, prayer, baptism and communion."[3] All of these worship moments written in the scripture can easily lend themselves to dance, enactment, or ritual. Much like William Shakespeare's plays were not meant to stay on the page but rather be brought to life on the stage, *The Bible* also has endless opportunities to be embodied through liturgical dance and other dramatic arts.

Mother and Child, Anita Davis, Ingrid Murphy, photo by Jane Wellford.

---

3. Taussig, "Dancing the Scriptures," 69.

CHAPTER 8

Worship Collaboration: Dancers Working with Clergy, Musicians, Readers of Text, and Staff

LITURGICAL DANCE IS ALMOST always a collaborative experience by its very intention and definition as dance within worship of the people. It is usually not an experience done in isolation, but with thoughtful intention in collaboration with others. Since liturgical dance often occurs within the liturgy itself, the dancer is working with clergy, musicians, church staff, and church laity to bring the worship experience to fruition. On other occasions when sharing dances of worship outside of the liturgy, liturgical dancers may work with a site director, a producer, other performers, designers, and technicians involved in the collaborative process. When dance is used within worship, it can be a very delicate mission to accomplish. There may be misperceptions, pre-conceived ideas that are desired but sometimes impossible, or even egos that may get in the way. Just saying aloud the two thematic ideas to be joined, worship and dance, gives some people a rise in pulse. For this joint venture to work smoothly toward a positive outcome for the worship community, pre-planning and collaboration with everyone involved are important.

An initial meeting early with those leading the worship event is necessary several months or at least several weeks prior to the event. This initial meeting may involve one or all of the following

Worship Collaboration

people to meet with the director or choreographer of the liturgical dance group: the minister or church worship leader, the director of music ministries, and the head of the host church's worship committee. Each one of these individuals brings with them their perceptions (real or imagined), creative ideas, and knowledge in their areas of expertise, as well as possible baggage. The clergy have spent years in seminary working on their theology degrees in preparation to lead their "flock." The dancers, choreographers, and musicians have spent years of training honing their art, many of them high-level professionals with graduate degrees. It is important to remember that the clergy, musicians, staff, and members of the host church have created an existing worship environment that works well for them. They are taking a growth step, as well as a risk, by inviting dance into their worship. I make this statement because I have been on both sides. Being married to a Presbyterian minister, I often put on the alter ego of a minister and think about issues a minister might consider since I have witnessed this first hand over the years, sharing with great empathy. Dancer and mime artist Sheila Kerrigan shares the following comments from her book, *The Performers Guide to the Collaborative Process*:

> Making art requires physical, emotional, and spiritual commitment as well as vulnerability and trust. Artists need to feel safe enough to move freely, experience feelings, and express themselves without fear of negative consequences. Everyone in a group holds the responsibility for maintaining a safe environment.[1]

Everyone present in the organizational process, clergy, musicians, and dancers, would ideally aim for a collaborative outcome that would work toward a "safe environment" for everyone, including the body of worshippers. In the choices made at initial meetings, I would hope that such additional goal outcomes as *inspirational, thought-provoking,* and *life-enhancing* would also be discussed in addition to goals of "safe environment" for everyone as planning proceeds.

1. Kerrigan, *Performer's Guide to the Collaborative Process*, 86-87.

PART II—Laying the Foundation for Liturgical Dance

My Spirit Soars, Emerson Bennett, photo by Anna Varnadoe.

Clergy, musicians, dancers, and worship committee members will all have questions dealing with everything from spacing in the sanctuary to placement of the dance in the order of worship, music to be used, and other valid questions. It is important to communicate any and all questions as a starting point for discussion, remembering that each worship experience is uniquely different depending on people, worship styles, denominations, physical spaces, and any past experiences that may color the future opportunities.

Worship Collaboration

Dancers Working with Musicians

In my collaborative work with musicians, it has been both a privilege and a pleasure to bring the marriage of dance with music to its best potential. Most of my experiences have been positive and have enhanced the liturgical dances far beyond my artistic, spiritual, or emotional expectations. A choreographer may choose to use music that is live or pre-recorded depending on many things: the host church or worship community's policy or tradition, what is available in a particular musical arrangement, and what is available in the way of resources. If a choreographer has the opportunity to work with musicians who will play "live" for you, by all means, go this route. Many organists, pianists, vocalists, and other musicians welcome this opportunity to work with a choreographer. It is important that the choreographer and the musicians collaborate thoroughly on the intended outcome.

Early in the process, it is necessary for the director of music ministries to supply the choreographer with a rehearsal recording and the sheet music of any intended musical arrangement for the worship service. It is important that the recorded music include any introduction, interludes, "amen," and tempo preferences if these are part of the musical arrangement as it will occur in the service.

The recording and sheet music could be sent by internet, or the music shared as a cd. The music should be provided for the choreographer months or at least weeks in advance of the event so that the creation of the dance may begin. The choreography may take weeks or months to create, and the dance rehearsals will take more time beyond the choreographic process.

Only on a couple of occasions has my liturgical dance troupe encountered awkward experiences when working with live music. On one occasion, a musician broke into an old habit of playing bridges between stanzas that were not on the dancer's rehearsal copy given to the choreographer by the musician. The musician did not realize that choreographers choreograph specific movements for *every* note or musical phrase given them. In a well-choreographed and rehearsed dance, dancers are never expected to just *wing it* up front in the sanctuary if the music is not the way it was originally given to the choreographer. This might be satisfactory for soloists who are seasoned and can improvise on the spot. However, for medium to large groups of dancers, this is real sabotage. Because dance is visual, *everything* shows. When a congregation sees dancing stop and hears the music continue, guess who the viewers think is in error? The dancers! The visual impact often overrides the auditory for a lasting impression, whether good or bad.

When dancing in worship to accompaniment of live music with or without vocalists, it is important to have a conversation with the musicians and vocalists ahead of time regarding the following important questions or points that will most likely need to be addressed.

1. What is the name of the music, the composer, and the particular arrangement being used for everyone involved in this collaboration?

2. How many stanzas are in this particular arrangement of music? If the music is a hymn, church hymnals are all quite different, even within the same denomination. It is important to ask about the number of stanzas in the hymn as well as the particular arrangement.

3. Will the musician play an introduction to the hymn or the anthem? If so, will the introduction be an entire stanza, an improvisation, or a few measures?

4. Will the musician be playing interludes, bridges, or improvisations between stanzas? Will there be any embellishment or a coda at the end of the music?

5. Will the tempo remain the same throughout the musical selection, including the introduction and the final stanza?

6. Will the hymn or anthem have an "amen" at the end?

7. If dancing to a processional or recessional, will there be others processing/recessing into or out of the sanctuary with the dancers during the singing of the hymn? Often there are

Worship Collaboration

ministers, liturgists, choirs, acolytes, crucifers, and others within the worship who may be involved in a processional or recessional in addition to the liturgical dancers. This is a very important point of clarification because choreographers choreograph steps to *all* the music. If there are additional people within the processional or recessional space, the entire dance will come out wrong if the inclusion of unknown *others* is not planned for choreographically in advance.

8. If using live music, when may the dancers have a rehearsal with the musicians prior to the worship event? This is important whether it happens days before the service, or the morning of the service prior to the worshippers entering the sanctuary. Timing, phrasing, mood, and everything matter when working in collaboration with music and movement. It is simply a must that this occurs with musicians and dancers prior to the worship event. (Also found in *Chapter 5: The Director of Liturgical Dance*)

9. If using pre-recorded music, make certain the use of pre-recorded music is acceptable with the host church or worship community. Some churches have a policy or tradition against pre-recorded music within their worship while others see this as a non-issue. If the liturgical dance group's repertory dances use pre-recorded music, and the host church does not allow pre-recorded music, ask the host church if the musicians and/or singers can provide live music to which the dancers might perform. If the answer is "yes," ask the host church to send the choreographer a copy of the music the church will be creating for you so that your dancers and the church musicians will be rehearsing to the same musical arrangement.

PART II—Laying the Foundation for Liturgical Dance

I Am Listening, Amy Wagoner, photo by Randy Piland.

10. If using pre-recorded music in a church setting, make sure the recording is of high-quality and test your music in the host church sound system prior to use. Sometimes host churches have out-of-date sound systems which are not effective if they usually use live music within worship. If the music played through a poor-quality sound system sounds bad, then the liturgical dance will be diminished as well. Using poor-quality pre-recorded music causes the viewers to work twice as hard to understand something the dancers or other leaders in worship are trying to make easy for them. Bring in a sound system if necessary.

11. Regarding choices of music, try to avoid using heavily orchestrated music for small groups of dancers. Heavily orchestrated music is not suited for small numbers of liturgical dancers sharing in worship. Large music requires large numbers of dancers and usually a large space to fill its volume, dynamics, and imaginings of more than a few dancers.

12. Avoid using music where the vocals are difficult to understand or where the music overpowers the words if your choreography is trying to interpret lyrics within the music. Not all music is well suited for liturgical dance. Sometimes

Worship Collaboration

worship music is better listened to for its own sake, without adding the additional dimension of movement. Choosing *not* to add liturgical dance to music may be the best choice in the following cases:

a. When the tempo is too fast and the dance movement looks suddenly irreverent or awkward within the dance and its setting.

b. When the music is too highly orchestrated or complex and may overpower anything additional, such as movement.

c. When the liturgical dance director has only one or two dancers and there is very large music such as large choir and orchestra, the music tends to overpower the dancers. Large music requires at least 6-8 or perhaps dozens of dancers to co-exist in partnership with the music. As a rule, it is recommended to have a soloist dancing to a solo vocalist or instrumentalist, a duet dancing when a duet is sung or performed instrumentally, etc.

d. If the words are not clearly audible to those *listening*, then the choreographed movements the congregation is *seeing* will be difficult to understand as well. Clarity on the part of both music and dance is imperative if clear communication and understanding are to be received by the worshipping community.

There are always options if the host church insists on using the music the choreographer has been given to work with for a particular worship event. The choreographer may ask that the tempo be slowed down or speeded up if the tempo needs adjusting. It could be as simple as asking for another arrangement of the music if the particular version is inappropriate for the dancers' abilities or other circumstance. There are often multiple arrangements of musical works that may be used as alternatives. It is always about working in collaboration to find the best solution.

PART II—Laying the Foundation for Liturgical Dance

Dancers Working with Readers of Text

Liturgical dance using text is often a welcomed experience within worship. The text may come in the form of the scripture for the day, a prayer, a poem, a parable, a psalm, or other texts. It is important to choose a good reader, male or female, who has a clear, articulate, and resonant speaking voice. Performing dances with text is similar to performing dances with music. Like music, text readings have rhythm, timing, pauses, inflections, and other unique characteristics. A rehearsal with the reader of the text is imperative prior to the worship event for optimal performance of the two art forms in tandem.

If scripture is the text to be read, it is important to check with the worship leader about the particular translation to be used within the service. Before the choreographer creates any movements for the text, the choreographer, the worship leader, and the reader need to use the same translation. Example: *New Revised Standard Version* of the scripture, or *King James Version*? There is a big difference in the choice of wording in different translations. Movements choreographed from different translations may have different choreographic outcomes and may cause differences in the interpretations of the viewers. After determining which scripture translation will be used, it is a good idea to create two master copies of the reading: one for the choreographer from which she creates the material and directs the dancers, and one for the reader of the text. Both copies should be exactly the same, complete with asterisks or other symbols denoting pauses where necessary within the reading where the dancers need extra time for movements.

Suggestions for Liturgical Dance Using Text

1. *Dance during the reading of the text.* This is the most common way of choreographing dances using text. It is fairly simple and may be used to interpret the scripture readings or other text for any worship service. As in dancing to music with lyrics, the reader must work out the timing and pauses

with the dancer during a few rehearsals. There is sometimes the temptation for the dancer to pantomime the words as the reader is reading. I encourage the dancer to try to use at least a little abstraction of movement at times rather than all literal interpretive movement as the text is read. During the rehearsal process, the dancer may ask the reader for pauses where dancing may continue if necessary. There needs to be an understanding of the dancer to artistically highlight certain main words within the reading, but not every word of the text, as this could be quite overdone.

2. *Dance after the text is read.* This is like reading the book and then seeing the movie! It is a delayed reinforcement using the visual following the auditory. Example: For a particular Advent service, I choreographed the following experience. The dancers stood in various locations throughout the chancel holding candles in a dimly lit evening service while reading Isaiah 9:2, 6. I had taken editorial liberties for various readers, who were also the dancers, to speak in unison, repetition, and canon. At the end of the reading, the dancers blew out their candles, put them down, and came forward into the chancel where they danced Isaiah's prophesy to a beautiful instrumental version from Handel's *Messiah*, *Unto Us a Child Is Born*. It was an incredibly moving experience as this Advent candlelight service revealed the word of God first through text, then followed by and reinforced with music and dance.

3. *Dance, text, and music occurring simultaneously.* This is often the most powerful way to use text, using three artistic dimensions at the same time, two auditory and one visual, to bring the worship experience to its highest sensory potential. Our dance troupe has had many successful experiences with this artistic blend of dancing, reading of text, and instrumental music together. Two examples of this are below. In both cases it was imperative that the reader of the text used a strong speaking voice with quality amplification over the orchestration in this collaboration of dance, text, and music.

PART II—Laying the Foundation for Liturgical Dance

    a. *Magnificat*: One summer at a Montreat Worship and Music Conference in Black Mountain, North Carolina, our liturgical dancers had the opportunity to dance John Ferguson's musical and spoken arrangement of *Magnificat*. During the music, a narrator read Mary's story from Luke 1:26-33, 38-42. Liturgical dance was shared during the music and the reading as the visual aid for the danced story, all at the same time.

    b. *God's Trombones*: Dance, music and text were used simultaneously again in another Montreat Worship and Music Conference by our dancers in a sharing of *God's Trombones*. A narrator read the story of James Weldon Johnson's *The Creation,* an interpretation of chapter 1 from the book of Genesis in *The Bible*. During the reading, the music of *God's Trombones* was performed on the organ while the Genesis creation story was danced and enacted to complement the words and music through movement, creating a powerful multi-sensory worship experience.

Dancers Working with Clergy and Church Staff

When working with clergy or worship leaders, the liturgical dancer is often an invited guest participant at a church other than her own. The dancer needs to know as much information as possible about the host group's worship style and structure prior to taking on any leadership role within worship. Background information and some history of the church or worship group are important to ask of the church's worship leader. The church's worship leader would be able to share information with the dancer about whether the church is Catholic, Protestant, or non-denominational, particular worship style of the church, the governing body of the church, past history of liturgical dance in worship, congregational make up, and above all, why liturgical dance has been invited within worship at this time. If this particular worship leader is new to this church, what is the prior history of using artists within worship before his or her time as worship leader?

It is a good idea for the dancer to discuss ideas and interpretation about the scripture or other text to be used within worship with the worship leader prior to choreographing for collaborative worship. Important insights or questions could be covered at this time. Other important questions to ask the clergy and worship committee are found in *Chapter 4: The Host Church or Worship Community*.

If the director of the liturgical dancers has any educational and/or promotional materials regarding liturgical dance, it is a good idea to share these with the church staff in advance of the worship event, especially if this is the first time liturgical dance has been shared at this location. Some information may be printed in the bulletin as an insert, or in the church newsletter ahead of time prior to the worship event. These steps are necessary since they are an opportunity for communication and enhanced understanding between the liturgical dancer and the worship community. Advance work in promoting liturgical dance prior to the event is important to quell any possible misunderstandings about what is going to occur. Some specific suggestions for possible information to share with the host church, prior to sharing in their worship may include the following:

History of liturgical dance in the Christian faith

Biblical passages where dance is cited in scripture

Literature that supports arts in worship, particularly dance

Biography of the director of the dance troupe and background of the dancers

Photographs that may be available of the dancers sharing in worship settings

Articles about liturgical dance that enhance public understanding

Terminology of liturgical dance

PART II—Laying the Foundation for Liturgical Dance

These are just a few of the many ways collaboration and information sharing may occur for those working to bring liturgical dance in worship to an effective outcome for everyone involved. When working together, clergy, musicians, dancers, readers, church staff, and other artists have endless possibilities to provide multi-dimensional collaborative worship experiences towards enhancement of a more dynamic worshipping community.

PART III

Practical Areas Regarding Liturgical Dance

CHAPTER 9

Space: Give Those Dancers an Inch and They'll Take an Aisle!

"SPACE, THE FINAL FRONTIER," said William Shatner, also known as Captain Kirk, first Captain of the Starship Enterprise at the beginning of every television episode and later films of *Star Trek*. I agree with Kirk that space is certainly a frontier and one of the most important *final frontiers* to conquer when working collaboratively within the confines of a church sanctuary. A *frontier* is "the border between two countries; limits of attainment or knowledge in a subject."[1] I could not agree more. I have often felt like space had "limits of attainment" when working in collaboration with some "powers that be" in churches and worship communities.

As an artist, my experience of working with ministers, musicians, and choirs has most often been extremely positive and productive. I have on occasion been challenged when I felt as if I was on "the border between two countries," or one of us had "limits of knowledge in our subject." This was usually due to lack of preparation or naivety on one part or the other. This occurred only on rare occasions and only in my beginning years as a liturgical dancer. When it did, it was a tremendous learning experience which I wish to pass along as a future pitfall for others to avoid.

Dancers in the secular area of concert dance usually have the luxury of a large square or rectangular stage space on which to

---

1. Jewell, *Oxford American Desk Dictionary and Thesaurus*, 324.

PART III—Practical Areas Regarding Liturgical Dance

perform their art. In liturgical dance, the spatial choices often do not remotely resemble this luxury. The space is usually a shared space of the chancel, aisle, or transept with many variables such as people and structures. The early Christian church was originally designed for worship leaders to orate and the main body of worshippers to stand and listen. Only centuries later did worship needs dictate changes to add pews and other seating areas. Still, much later were public address systems and acoustic needs for worshippers considered and implemented.

It was not until the 1960s that new spacious worship centers began to include more space for visual and performing arts. During this time, noticeable changes in both church architecture as well as worship styles began to emerge. In the late 1970s, large worship centers and mega-churches began to appear. From the 1980's and into the twenty-first century, many traditional church structures underwent renovations to accommodate changing worship trends, often with the inclusion of space for performing arts in worship. It became more common to find dance, drama, puppetry, mime, visual arts, power point visuals and lighting projections among other technological advances in worship.

Still, many sanctuaries simply do not have adequate space for liturgical dance or other dramatic arts. Churches and worship centers are expensive to build and cannot afford to rebuild each time worship trends change. However, some churches do renovate their sanctuary spaces to accommodate new and growing worship trends. Many worship leaders make the best of their existing spaces and church budgets to keep up with changing trends while meeting the needs of their congregations.

Whether a church's existing structure does or does not have adequate space should not limit creative ideas for the many worship possibilities available. Those who work in the church should not let the space define what they *think* their church is able to do regarding worship arts. In thinking about worship possibilities, a good idea is to get someone to sit beside you out in the nave of the sanctuary and look at the worship space while you brainstorm possible ideas together. Many wonderful visual and performing

Space: Give Those Dancers an Inch and They'll Take an Aisle!

arts are able to be incorporated within worship in small and often dated sanctuary spaces. Another option is that the worship event involving liturgical dance could happen in a neighboring church that has the best spatial facility, resulting in a community event where several churches join together.

Macedonia Lutheran Church, Burlington, NC, photo by Jane Wellford.

Artists who make the commitment to go into churches and share the word of God through dance or other dramatic arts must learn collaboration skills in order to adapt to frequent spatial issues and constraints. Worship spaces come in a variety of styles and options, just like ice cream flavors. Host churches will most often give-and-take with worship artists regarding their spatial needs. The artist must simply ask for space and remind the host church that dance and other dramatic arts are visual enhancements to worship and must be seen to be successful in worship. Allowances will most often be made when furnishings and structures can be moved and placed right back into their original spaces following or sometimes during the service.

Using liturgical dance or other worship arts is capable of being an amazing experience for everyone involved when the creative efforts of clergy, artists, technicians, and laity planning the experience communicate well during the process. Mistakes

PART III—Practical Areas Regarding Liturgical Dance

will occasionally occur regardless of careful planning. But the enhancement of worship possibilities is often worth it for those who receive this multi-sensory visual and auditory worship experience. Working collaboratively, clergy and liturgical dancers sharing space in worship is where creative ideas may range from simple to complex depending upon what is to be shared and congregational needs. It is a matter of heartfelt discussion and focused vision to know when to stir the existing waters and when to stay on the shore. Trying on new worship styles in old or new worship spaces takes courage and needs to be entered into with prayer, discussion, and education on the part of everyone involved.

My father-in-law once told me that he did not know everything. I found this hard to believe when I was younger, naïve, and newly married to his son. After all, he was older and wiser and had amassed great wisdom over his years as a successful attorney. Then he added that he *did* know to ask others for the answers when he did not know the answers himself and that this was one of the greatest assets to his success.

The trouble with most of us is that we just don't ask the questions. If we cannot imagine ourselves doing something or knowing about something, then it must not be within our realm of possibility. But what about our daily lives, our worship practices, or our very spirits? Do these need enhancement? Do we deny ourselves or others the possibility for growth due to our own often limited visions? If we are to take our worship seriously, then we may need to look beyond the limits of our personal and spatial vision. It is easy to see the same space before us every Sunday rather than the worship possibilities that *might* occur within the space. Why not begin to look into possibilities of enhancing worship and making it applicable for everyone, not only certain faithful pew warmers? If the vision is not ours, then it just might be someone else's. Others may have suggestions even if we don't. Like the example of my wise father-in-law, we all have the potential to be better informed and see things from another's perspective. We must humble ourselves to take the first step and perhaps simply ask.

Space: Give Those Dancers an Inch and They'll Take an Aisle!

A look at the physical space

Although liturgical dance may occur in many locations, church sanctuaries, fellowship halls, auditoriums, retreat and conference centers are still the most common locations for this worship art to be performed. Let us look at the interior structure of many sanctuary spaces. Aisles, pews or chairs, and a chancel or stage area upfront are pretty standard in many sanctuaries or worship spaces. Therefore, I will address space issues related within this most common structural format.

The *aisles*, the *transept*, and the *chancel* area within a sanctuary are the three main areas where dance in worship most commonly takes place. All three of these spatial areas are defined as follows:

Aisle—The open path walking area (which may have steps) between rows of pews or other sitting areas.[2] This area allows worshippers entrance and exit possibilities within the sanctuary.

St. Mark's Church, Burlington, NC, photo by Jane Wellford.

Transept—Either arm of a cross-shaped church (gothic architecture) at right angles to the nave, or seating area, of the sanctuary.

2. Ibid., 19.

PART III—Practical Areas Regarding Liturgical Dance

The crossing space or walking area, between the front pew and the often up-raised chancel area. This spatial floor area is often about five to six feet deep and extends in width beyond the nave of the church into the side wing space in front of the worship space.[3] If one visualizes this area of the worship space as that of a cross-shaped architectural design, then the transept space is the crossbar where Christ's arms are wide open and outstretched, reaching side to side. Liturgical dancers often dance in this area but may be visually seen only from the waist up, since most transept areas are on the ground level.

Chancel—Part of a church near the altar.[4] This is often a slightly elevated level of floor space upfront in a sanctuary. Within this space, one might find an altar, a communion table and walking space for clergy or other worship leaders. Other items commonly found within this space might include a pulpit, a lectern, an organ or a piano, a baptismal font and possibly flower stands. In more contemporary worship spaces, one might find electric keyboards, drum sets, microphone stands, and amplifiers. Choirs are sometimes seated or standing within or to the sides of this area. Worshippers in a church sanctuary are usually facing this area, and the worship leaders are facing the congregation from this area as they lead the worship service.

Dance, like stained glass windows, tapestries, sculptures, dramas, power point visuals, or other visual arts used in worship, must be *seen* in worship to be effective. One can hear beautiful music and powerful sermons within worship even with eyes closed. But one must open one's eyes and have clear sight lines to receive the visual arts. If liturgical dance is shared where only half of the body is visible, then clear communication of the danced message is not able to take place. I compare this experience to looking at a piece of sculpture or a painting where half of the work of art is covered with a drape. Would we cover half of Michelangelo's sculpture of

3. Ibid., 892.
4. Ibid., 124.

Space: Give Those Dancers an Inch and They'll Take an Aisle!

the *Pieta*, or half of Leonardo Da Vinci's *The Last Supper* and ask those viewing to fully grasp the meaning of each? Would we limit the organist or pianist use of only the white keys on the keyboard to perform Beethoven's *Ode to Joy*? Just like sculpture, painting, or music, liturgical dance, when denied full visibility within worship, allows the receiver only half of the communication experience, from the waist up. To have half of the message distorted or "draped" by poor visibility within most sanctuaries is certainly not the best way for this worship art to be experienced. Therefore, the dance, or other visual worship arts, must be fully visible to be seen. Full visibility could be improved by dancing in an elevated chancel area, placing platforms in the transept, or by performing on a stage within a worship space that offers this option.

Chapter 1 informs us that dance must have four main elements to occur, one of the main elements being *space*. Music, rhythm, and even excellent technique are actually secondary elements for dance to occur, but *space* is absolutely necessary for dance to be shared.

On one particular occasion during Advent, I was asked to choreograph Benjamin Britten's *Ceremony of Carols*. This was to be performed for a series of three evening worship concerts in a large gothic church in Greensboro, North Carolina. Within this particular experience, I served as both choreographer and as one of the ten dancers, working in collaboration with two choirs, several musicians, and two conductors. I was asked to choreograph a total of eight different dances which involved a time commitment of six months to create and rehearse. Since the choirs and musicians were to occupy three-fourths of the chancel area (which was upraised and had perfect sightlines), there was almost no room for the dances to take place, much less be viewed by those in attendance. Therefore, the dancers, sharing the visual component of the worship experience, would be able to be seen only from the waist up, performing in the transept space. After surveying the potential of the sanctuary space, I decided to ask that platforms be brought in to the open side spaces of the transept to elevate the dance and allow for clear visibility of choirs, musicians and dancers. This way,

PART III—Practical Areas Regarding Liturgical Dance

those viewing and listening could have optimal viewing and optimal hearing of what was occurring within worship—a true multi-sensory experience. After months of choreography and rehearsals, I ended up using all available spatial areas in the sanctuary. The dancing took place on the platforms, in the aisles, in the transept area, on the steps going up into the chancel area, and the remaining one-fourth area of the chancel near the musicians and choirs. It turned out to be an excellent experience for everyone participating and worshipping in the services. The outcome was a positive one due to extensive preparation of all artists working in collaboration.

First Lutheran Church, Greensboro, NC,
photo by Jane Wellford.

One very important piece of advice regarding space in collaborative work between the host church and dancers: visit the host church *prior to* doing any choreography. Walk around and measure the space where any dance will take place. If the host church is too far a distance away for an on-site visit, ask the host church to digitally send, mail, or fax a photo of the sanctuary space or other location where the dance will occur. Always ask for sanctuary measurements of aisles, transepts, and chancel space with the photos if you can't be present in the space ahead of time.

Space: Give Those Dancers an Inch and They'll Take an Aisle!

Dancing in the Aisles

The aisles are commonly used by dancers for processionals and recessionals, coming from either the front or the back of the sanctuary. Dancing in the aisles is visible by everyone present within the space. Most church sanctuaries have at least one to three aisles, and many contemporary churches have as many as ten or more aisles. Photos of sanctuary spaces are included within this chapter displaying aisles, transepts, and chancels where dance and other worship arts often occur.

St. Andrews-Covenant Presbyterian Church, Wilmington, NC,
photo courtesy of Sharon Miller.

When dancing in the aisles, liturgical dancers sometimes carry banners or flags. Performing with props such as these, the dancer must be aware of the width of each aisle in order not to touch, or accidentally hit, members of the congregation with props during processions or recessions. Dancers should take into consideration the height of the seated or standing worshippers in the pews when processing with flags or banners. When entering aisles with flags or banners, dancers should always raise these props high into the vertical space. On a particular Easter Sunday, I saw a lady almost lose her hat due to an over-zealous dancer using flags

97

PART III—Practical Areas Regarding Liturgical Dance

during a processional. On another occasion, one of my dancers almost caught a flag on fire when swirling it too near lighted candles on a communion table!

Sometimes, regardless of advance planning, life happens in the form of unexpected obstacles. One such "obstacle situation" occurred early in my career as a liturgical dancer. On a particular Reformation Sunday in a Lutheran Church in Greensboro, North Carolina, a member of the church (not on the worship planning committee) placed Pennies for Hunger Baskets in the aisles just before the opening processional hymn, *A Mighty Fortress Is Our God*. Although our dancers had just completed a final spacing rehearsal one hour earlier where no obstacles were in sight, several medium size baskets had suddenly been placed in the aisles right before the opening processional hymn. Additionally, the choir director suddenly decided to place a large wooden podium in the aisle and stood in front of it to direct the choir. These unexpected obstacles were right in our dancing path and it was too late to make any changes. On one of my turns down the aisle during this opening hymn, I accidentally knocked over the wooden podium during a turn, scattering sheet music in all directions. The scene looked like snow flurries within a ten foot radius! The choir director tried to catch the podium, but it was too late, like watching a car wreck in slow motion. In addition, the Pennies for Hunger baskets had gotten tangled up under the robes of the dancers as they turned. Subtle laughter could be heard as we neared verse four of the processional hymn. My hand was beginning to throb from striking the podium. What kind of Murphy's Law service was this, and we had two more dances to share in the service! When the service finally did end, my dancers and I quickly headed for the parking lot, embarrassed by the sabotage that had occurred within what we thought was a carefully planned worship event. Near the end of the week, I received a nice letter from the pastor of the church, thanking our troupe for our participation in that Reformation Day service. To my surprise, the letter was written with much joy. "Thank

Space: Give Those Dancers an Inch and They'll Take an Aisle!

you for a festive and moving interpretation of *A Mighty Fortress Is Our God*. After this first hymn, one of our younger members of the church said out loud, 'Wow! That was neat!' We look forward to having you again soon."[5] Who knew? Nothing of that magnitude has occurred since, and our dancers have returned to share dance in that Lutheran church on other occasions. The minister and I remain friends to this day.

Dancing in the Transept

When liturgical dance is shared in front of those worshipping in the transept area, there is usually a sight-line problem. The front transept area of a church is often a flat base rather than an upraised area like the chancel or a stage. Therefore, only the top half of the liturgical dancer's body is visible. Unlike centuries ago in the early Christian church where worshippers stood, worshippers remain seated during most of the worship service today. Since liturgical dancers share their dances on the same level of space as those viewing, whole body visibility of the dancer is not possible in the transept. Because of this, when dances of worship occur in the transept, the choreographer needs to place most of the movement and focus emphasis on the upper body.

As a choreographer, I generally use the transept space for processional and recessional dances. After the dancers enter the sanctuary by way of the aisles, they often continue dancing throughout the rest of the hymn within the transept or chancel space. The reverse is true for recessional dances. In recessionals, the dancers begin in the chancel or transept space, dance throughout the hymn or anthem in this space, and then recess down the aisles of the nave towards the narthex to exit on the final verses of the hymn.

Due to this visibility challenge, the dancer must engage the *communal presence* posture when dancing in the transept. *Communal presence* posture is mentioned in complete detail earlier in

---

5. Zimmerman, Thank you letter from pastor of First Lutheran Church, 1991

PART III—Practical Areas Regarding Liturgical Dance

Chapter 3: Intention in Liturgical Dance. This lifted and welcoming upper body posture is the invitational presence, focus, and expression that the dancer uses to communicate best when performing in this spatial area. Since so much of liturgical dance in churches occurs in the *transept*, the upper body *communal presence* is an important technique for communication used by the liturgical dancer.

If some of the traditional church architecture and church furnishings become too restrictive of a space for the dancers, the liturgical dance director may have to do one of two things: change the choreography, or request the worship committee to allow the worship dance to be performed in an alternate location such as a fellowship hall or a community reception room.

Dancing in the Chancel

Because the chancel area of space is often elevated, the chancel is usually the best location for sharing liturgical dance in a worship space. Some churches have a stage which is definitely optimal for viewing visual presentational arts in worship. Everything the choreographer has created shows clearly when set user-friendly in a raised chancel area, stage, or platform. Some church chancel spaces are larger and more accessible for dancers than others. An elevated space allows more choreographic freedom of the dancers movements since all levels of movement are clearly visible from head to toe. Choreography for dance performed in an elevated space affords the luxury of using all three levels of spatial movement possibilities (low = movements close to the floor, middle = medium level lunges or bows, and high = leaps, turns, jumps, arabesques, etc.).

Space: Give Those Dancers an Inch and They'll Take an Aisle!

Elon Community Church, Elon, NC, photo by Jane Wellford.

If the liturgical dancer needs items within this space moved away or pushed back, the dancer should *first* and *always* ask permission from the host church. Moving church furnishings is sometimes not an option. Many items with regard to church furnishings, particularly in the chancel, are sometimes treated as "sacred cows" and have a long and often emotional history with members of the congregation. "My Aunt Mary gave that baptismal font to the church as a memorial when Uncle Henry died and it is not to be moved—ever!" And the list goes on. Again, a gentle reminder for respect and give-and-take between the guest worship participants and the host church. Dancers must always remember they are often invited guests within each house of worship they share. However, if a church chooses to invite liturgical dancers to be part of the worship service, then please allow the dancers space to do what they were invited to do—share the word of God through movement to enhance the worship. It is all relative to the particular situation where the give-and-take is managed regarding the space.

In some instances, small changes within the chancel space may be necessary to allow liturgical dance to occur that are usually within reason. For example, the baptismal font may be moved right back to its original place before the next service, or the

PART III—Practical Areas Regarding Liturgical Dance

communion table may even be moved forward or back before communion within the same service. A liturgical dance is a sharing of the words through movement, just like the sermon, the anthems, prayers, and hymns. The only difference is that the worship art of dance is visual, takes up space, and must be seen in order to be effective. The choreographer may have to change or adapt the choreography after learning what she can and cannot move regarding church furnishings. If adjustments are unable to be made to the space to improve visibility, then the dancers should do their best within the space they are given.

Our liturgical dance troupe has often had to re-choreograph entire dances at a spacing rehearsal in a sanctuary prior to the sharing within worship. Many of the low-level movements had to be changed to middle-level or high-level movements for the dancers' movements to be visible to the congregation. Sometimes it is like having to re-write portions of a symphony when liturgical dancers must re-choreograph a work they have been rehearsing for months due to spatial constraints within a sanctuary. I have often said jokingly that liturgical dancers must be able to dance in a space the size of a postage stamp! This next spatial experience was close to a postage stamp but more like a tiered wedding cake. Rather than a spatial problem of dancing around objects, it was a problem of unique church architecture.

The Wedding Cake Chancel!

On one occasion, our dancers were asked to perform in a large Lutheran Church in Burlington, North Carolina in a fairly traditional sanctuary interior. There was one marked difference with regard to the chancel area. It looked like a white marble, multi-tiered wedding cake! We had been asked to share five dances of worship for a Wednesday evening Lenten service. Fortunately, we had arrived the day before the event for a two hour afternoon spacing rehearsal. Unfortunately, we had not asked for a photograph of the worship space or visited the site ahead of time. As we entered the sanctuary, we gazed up at the chancel, gasped, put on

Space: Give Those Dancers an Inch and They'll Take an Aisle!

our warm-ups, and began our work. The chancel area, where 90 percent of our dancing was to occur, was an albatross of a spacing issue. It only had three feet of flat space in the transept that fed into three marble steps up, two more feet of space, then finally another two steps up to a communion table platform with only two feet around on all sides. In addition, there was communion rail around the second "tier of the cake" that prevented movement up and down the steps. Whoa! Each of the five dances for this particular service had to be re-choreographed due to this spacing dilemma. The spacing rehearsal lasted from four in the afternoon until midnight that night! Our normal two-hour spacing rehearsal turned out to be eight hours. After this experience, we learned to look at every space, either live or in photographs, before agreeing to participate in worship events.

The Temporary Communion Rail That Stayed!

At another Lutheran Church in Virginia, we were absolutely surprised by a portable communion rail that stayed in place. On one particular Sunday at an eight-thirty morning service, our dancers had already shared three dances in this early service where communion rails were put into place, communion served, then the rails removed prior to the final prayer and the danced benediction. No spatial problems anywhere in sight. However, during the eleven o'clock service this same day, there was a different set of assistants to serve communion. This in itself did not present any problems for us since we knew the rails would go up and come down just like they did during the earlier service. We were to perform three *different* dances for the second morning service where the open and available communion space was crucial to accomplish the final dance. Just as in the earlier service, we bowed our heads to pray for the closing prayer before our recessional dance from the chancel area. Upon opening our eyes at the end of the prayer, we discovered the communion rails were still in place and the music for our dance had begun. The rails cut directly through the middle of our planned choreography for the dance, leaving us almost no

PART III—Practical Areas Regarding Liturgical Dance

room for six dancers with full robes and flags to move. We instantly had to think on our feet and second-guess each other's anticipated moves. It was terrifying, cluttered looking, and certainly not our best dance to end a worship service. As we occasionally whacked the communion rails with our flags and tried to smile and look pleasant in our crowded cubicle, the final stanza of the hymn that seemed to last forever finally concluded. This was yet another example that *everyone* involved in the worship service, including communion assistants at *both* services, needed to be involved in the planning of the worship.

Still today, I am amazed that such unexpected errors occur, regardless of infinite planning. To bring worship to its highest potential for the worshipping community, I still support the use of collaborative work between church personnel and incoming worship artists. It is worth the occasional bloopers of the unexpected.

CHAPTER 10

Costume Suggestions

IF LITURGICAL DANCE IS about communicating the Word of God through movement and is visual enhancement to worship, then what the dancer wears is an important decision to be given serious consideration. Costuming for liturgical dance has a wide range of possibilities. From church Christmas pageant stock to regular pedestrian clothing, the spectrum of possibilities is diverse. What, when, and where the liturgical dancer is sharing her dance has everything to do with costume choice.

If the dancer is performing a scripture reading from the *Bible* and wants to keep the content and theme of the dance traditional, then Christmas pageant stock costumes resembling clothing from the biblical time period might be appropriate. If the dancer is sharing a dance accompanied by a piece of contemporary Christian music, then pedestrian clothing or more stylized costuming may be appropriate. If the dancer is performing a ceremonial ritual dance within the liturgy, the dancer might choose to wear a chasuble robe or a long dress for a female, or robes over slacks for males, creating a more formal appearance.

In addition to choosing the appropriate costume for liturgical dance, the dancer needs to feel comfortable physically, mentally, and spiritually in what she is wearing before the worshipping community. If the dancer feels the least bit self-conscious, then attention will not be on dancing *the message* but on self. The feeling and sensitivity of the worshippers should certainly be taken

PART III—Practical Areas Regarding Liturgical Dance

into consideration also. Those witnessing should not be given any reason to feel uncomfortable or threatened by the dancer's appearance. Any costume choice that causes the performer or the worshipper to feel inadequate or compromised is a poor choice.

The question often arises as to how much of the dancer's body is to be revealed or how much to cover up. The dancer's costume should not be unnecessarily revealing, but at the same time, should not hide the lines of the body when it is encumbered by too many yards of fabric. It is a good rule not to have a costume too low in front, or revealing of too much bare leg when dancing within worship. Some liturgical dresses must be slit up one or both sides to the knee to allow for freedom of movement in the dance. In this case, tights or a unitard worn underneath the dress may be considered as an option if the dancer chooses. If the costume is too sheer or too tight, this could be a problem as well. Avoid Lycra fabric in costuming that is too thin or poorly fitting for the dancer. Lycra or cotton Lycra blend is a good fabric and is supposed to cling and be close to the body, but should not be *overly* tight. Bodies come in all shapes and sizes. Select costumes that are flattering to everyone in the group, not just the dancers who look good in everything.

Through teaching both secular dance and sacred dance, the costume choices I make in one area often do not apply in the other. Good judgment and common sense apply to both. Basically if a costume choice causes the worshipping community to stumble in their thinking or damage what is about to occur through the dance in worship, I will choose not to use that costume. It's all about enhancing worship, never distracting from it by making an inappropriate choice. Just because you have last year's recital costumes in your closet does not mean these same costumes will work for a worship service. Not everything secular can be transposed into the worship setting.

Costume Suggestions

Recessional Dance, Leigh Stanfill, photo by Kim Walker.

The choreography for Moving Liturgy Dance Ensemble ranges from contemporary to classical dances, formal to informal, serious to satirical, and many dance genres in between. We use everything from pedestrian clothing to highly formal costuming. Therefore, we keep a base of the following to use for just about all of our costume needs. Our material choices for costumes are tasteful and are of quality fabric. The following are our main costumes we have in stock for the majority of our repertory needs.

Black slacks of quality fabric, which flow fairly loose from the hips to the ankles.

Tunic tops in solid stained glass colors (blue, red, green, purple and gold) and another set in muted tones.

Sleeveless, non-contoured tops in black and in white that hang loosely to mid-hip in length. These may have a four inch slit in the sides for ease in movement.

Chasuble robes, much like a priest's robe, to wear over long dresses or black slacks. Our troupe's chasuble robes are in muted colors and another set in stained glass solid colors of green, rose, blue, purple, and pink.

Ankle-length dresses in stained glass colors and in muted colors made of quality thick, non-shiny Lycra. A unique feature about these dresses is that they have built in, ankle length legs under the skirt portion of the dress, much like a unitard, but all in one piece. These long sleeved dresses are high in the front with a boat neck, and have a scooped back down to mid-back. They are double-lined in the front.

Christmas Pageant Stock Disciple and Shepherd Costumes— These are easily made from the "angel costume" patterns in fabric stores. This costume is an ankle length pull over tunic with wrist-length bell shaped sleeves. Many churches have this type of costume in their Christmas pageant stock. I use this type of costume for dancers to dress like the disciples or perhaps Christ might have dressed 2,000 years ago. These are appropriate to wear when enacting biblical parables and teachings of Christ. Our stock of these costumes are in muted earth tone colors as well as stained glass colors and are slit up the sides to the knee for ease of movement. Often dresses or slacks are worn underneath. These costumes are usually worn with a long, black tie belt that hangs about eighteen inches down after being tied at the waist, worn over to the side.

Tunic Overlays—These are sheer, lightweight, sleeveless, knee-length tunic tops slit up each side to mid-thigh. These tunics are usually worn over a long, ankle length dress, or with black slacks and black camisole top or turtle neck top. Since the overlays are worn over a base dress or slacks, it is a good idea to contrast the darker base of pants or dress with a lighter colored tunic overlay, often the same color but a lighter shade.

The director of the liturgical dancers should be knowledgeable about colors of the church seasons prior to selecting and using costumes within worship. Specific colors remind us of the symbolic significance of special periods of the church's seasonal history.

Costume Suggestions

There are seven main seasons in the Christian Church: Advent, Christmas, Epiphany, Lent, Easter, Pentecost, and Ordinary Time. Each of the church seasons is represented by a particular color, although there are some variations in seasonal colors within certain church denominations. Advent is blue or purple, Christmas is white and sometimes gold, Epiphany is white, Lent is purple or violet, Easter is white, and Pentecost is red on the first Sunday and green for the rest of this season into Ordinary Time. On Good Friday, black is the prominent color or sometimes dark purple. The liturgical dancer should be mindful of these colors and, for example, should not wear black on such days as Easter Sunday or Christmas. Colors have a strong symbolic significance of which many church members are aware.

Teaching the Word, Betsy Reeves, Ingrid Murphy, Ginger Strickland, Jane Wellford, Anita Davis, photo by Bethany Cubino.

Sometimes liturgical dance groups have white dresses or white tops and black slacks in stock and wear them on every occasion for liturgical dance. This is certainly understandable for budgetary reasons and can be easily be enhanced with little expense. A simple tunic overlay or a sash of the church seasonal color may

PART III—Practical Areas Regarding Liturgical Dance

be added over the white dress or around the waist with slacks to make it even more meaningful and appropriate when the occasion calls for this variety.

Often youth groups perform in casual attire. Summer workshops, youth retreats, and youth Sundays are perfect times for youth involvement with movement and dance in worship. The youth might wear jeans and white t-shirts or black slacks and solid color tops to perform a dance in worship. On the first Sunday in Pentecost one year, our youth group wore jeans, white t-shirts, and small red ribbons on their shirts to represent the red color of Pentecost. They performed a dramatic reading of a litany they wrote, danced to the hymn *Pass It On,* and ended dancing a Pentecost prayer. It was a beautiful experience and all in pedestrian clothing. The church was fine with this costume choice and it worked well within this youth service portion of the service.

The age of the dancer is an important consideration in costume choice. I have had different ages of children perform *The Lord's Prayer* in their Sunday clothes up in the chancel during the service. On another occasion, the children wore their choir robes to perform a very simple dance/drama piece. One could put young children in just about anything and it would be fine. Sometimes it is necessary for them to look alike or be uniquely costumed, but at other times, nothing special is necessary.

In the case of older youth and adults, costume choices need a little more consideration. A good idea for checking dancer's costumes, even as simple as t-shirts, is that if the dancer raises her arms up high and her stomach skin shows, then the top needs to be longer. The liturgical dance director should be aware of clothing choices that are neither distracting nor embarrassing for the dancer or the worshippers, where midriff or cleavage might be exposed. The converse is sometimes the case in certain dancewear catalogues regarding the liturgical or praise dance section of costumes. Some liturgical dance costumes displayed in catalogues portray women in particular wearing volumes of material, sending a message that dancers should cover up from neck to ankle if they want to dance in worship. Again, it's all a matter of common sense.

Costume Suggestions

If the director wants to show the teachings of Jesus, the miracles of God, and the joys and sufferings we all share, please allow the dancer the opportunity and ability to move to communicate these concepts in their dances. Tasteful costumes should allow freedom of movement while shaping the general contour of the body without being too revealing. Conversely, costumes should not make the dancer look like they are wearing a tent!

Cost is often a consideration in costume choices. If choosing to order dancewear, props, or accessories for liturgical dance, the director might look online at websites under *liturgical dance, worship dance, praise dance,* or *lyrical dance*. See suggested websites below for possible options. If looking on-line is not your preferred search method, go to a local dance studio or dancewear store and ask to look through their dancewear and costume catalogues. Most dancewear catalogues have liturgical dancewear, props, and accessories under the same categories as mentioned above.

http://www.spiritualexpressions.com/dresses/default.aspx

http://www.dancewearsolutions.com/dance_styles/worship/default.aspx

http://www.worshipflagstore.com/praise-dancewear/

http://www.designsfordance.com/worship/default.aspx

http://www.discountdance.com/worship.php

http://www.reflectionsofdance.com/shop/dresses.html
http://baumsdancewear.com/category/Praiseworship.html

http://www.dfwga.com/home

Another option is to ask church members who might be interested in sewing and volunteering their time and talents to make costumes for you. I have found a wealth of costume makers in the following places: churches, fabric stores, dance studios, college dance or theatre arts programs, and parents or other relatives of liturgical dancers. I have often made my own chasuble robes from inexpensive full-size or queen-size solid color sheets from linen

PART III—Practical Areas Regarding Liturgical Dance

stores. I simply made a hole in the middle of the sheet for the head of the dancer to poke through and did little else.

Our Father, Heather Zachary, Katelyn Smith, Kaelyn Green, photo by Kim Walker.

The use of props when performing liturgical dance is fairly common. Props may come in the form of flags, streamers on short or tall fiber-glass rods, large Lycra bags for abstract *bag dances*, pieces of long fabric, or anything that may enhance communication

Costume Suggestions

in a dance of worship. Props are often used to complement storytelling of parables or other scripture passages and various worship songs. These props are also found in costume and dancewear catalogues and on the websites listed in this chapter by clicking on "accessories" or "props" for liturgical dance.

Make your own Worship Flags—Our liturgical dance troupe makes our own worship flags for formal and often general worship processional dances. We purchase inexpensive wooden dowels (one-half inch diameter by three feet in length) from a local home improvement store. Next we purchase inexpensive polysilk, polyester, taffeta, tissue lame, or anything that flows like silk in solid church seasonal colors or in bold stained glass colors. Then we cut the fabric in strips of forty-two inches in length and twelve to fourteen inches wide. We hem the edges of the fabric so it will not fray. Finally, we apply hot glue the length of the short end of the fabric to the dowel from the top to the end of the short end of the fabric. Then roll two inches of the short end of the fabric around the hot glue on the dowel, and hold it firm with our hands for five minutes, making sure the glue and the fabric have bonded to the dowel. Next, lay the dowel with the glued fabric flat to dry overnight, and it is ready for use the next morning. If you choose not to make your flags and would rather order them, an excellent website for worship flags is: http://www.worshipflagstore.com/worship-flags/.

To wear shoes or not to wear shoes when performing in a church sanctuary is sometimes a consideration. If you are sharing a dance wearing Biblical costumes such as those the disciples may have worn 2,000 years ago, then bare feet or dance sandals might be appropriate. Sometimes ballet shoes, jazz shoes, or even pointe shoes are appropriate with costumes, depending on the style or genre of dance to be performed. Often pedestrian clothing with pedestrian shoes is an appropriate choice when enacting contemporary stories of the Christian faith. It is important to consider the worship community with which you are sharing the dance. If the church is conservative or perhaps has never experienced liturgical dance prior to this time, then perhaps ballet slippers instead of bare

PART III—Practical Areas Regarding Liturgical Dance

feet in a processional entry down the aisle is an appropriate choice. I usually make the shoe decision after learning what the worship community is like. Sometimes it is a matter of safety for the dancers as to what they wear or do not wear on their feet. I have made the decision for my dancers not to wear shoes if a slate or wooden sanctuary floor is too slick or newly waxed for safety reasons.

In closing, choosing appropriate costuming when placing liturgical dance within worship is extremely important. I have seen an entire congregation turned off to liturgical dance even before the first movement occurred because of the dance director's poor choice of costuming. Handle this area with respect, sensitivity, and analysis far in advance before the worship experience for the sake of the dancers and the worship community.

CHAPTER 11

Fees: To Charge or Not To Charge?

SHOULD DANCERS OR CHOREOGRAPHERS charge a fee for liturgical dance in worship? Just like ministers *preach* the word of God, and members of the choir *sing* the word of God, the liturgical dancer *dances* the word of God. Some of these individuals get paid and some do this for gratis. Whether or not the dancer gets paid for her services as a liturgical dancer is dependent upon many things.

1. Whether the liturgical dancer is a professional dancer and a non-member invited into the church.
2. Whether the liturgical dancer is a member within the church and is doing this as part of their volunteer ministry like Sunday school teachers or choir members. Sometimes, there may be a professional liturgical dancer within the church who may expect to be paid.
3. The experience level of the liturgical dancer.
4. The extent of material asked to be choreographed and shared in worship: a simple processional hymn of three stanzas, an entire musical cantata in nine to twelve sections, or perhaps three to five dances within the liturgy.
5. Whether the liturgical dancer is sharing *within* the worship service, or performing a one-hour worship concert of sacred or liturgical dances on a Sunday afternoon or evening for the church and community.

PART III—Practical Areas Regarding Liturgical Dance

Early in my career and often today as a liturgical dancer, I have been paid and not paid. It was dependent upon many factors, such as the complexity and content of what was requested of me as a dancer/choreographer, and sometimes the size of the church. Usually, I did not charge for performances within my own church. However, when I brought my entire company to perform, I expected my church to pay my dancers because they were invited guests. Even after becoming established as a professional liturgical dancer, there are still occasions where I share my fee sheet for expenses, and many other times where it is a free sharing, depending on the situation.

Moving Liturgy Dance Ensemble has developed a fee scale that acts as a "suggested" guide for the liturgical dancer who is established. When Moving Liturgy drives or flies to certain locations, we expect the host church to pay for our gas or airfare, lodging, and food expenses. Because we are a professional dance troupe, a great deal of preparation, analysis of the music, text, choreography, and rehearsals have gone into the preparation of the dances of worship prior to arrival at the site. Upon site arrival, most often at a sanctuary, several hours are spent in a spacing rehearsal with the dancers. This is followed by one or more rehearsals with musicians and readers of text, followed by a final meeting with worship leaders of the service.

Much like a minister or a church musician who has invested a great deal of time and expense in their education and training, a professional dancer has done this as well. Please note the following procedures that occur when a liturgical dancer is requested to create and produce a new work for a church liturgy or worship concert. This is simply a reminder to the host group of the services the church is paying for when hiring a liturgical dancer or an entire dance troupe to share in worship as guests in a church or worship community.

Fees: To Charge or Not To Charge?

The Job of the Director of the Liturgical Dance Ensemble

1. Meet with the host church to determine what parts of liturgy are to be "danced" regarding musical compositions or text readings.

2. Obtain photographs and measurements for the spacing where the dance will take place. Since dance is spatial, taking space measurements is a must before any choreography is begun. The liturgical dancer's movement space is often filled with levels of steps, communion rails, baptismal fonts, lecterns, communion tables, pianos, bell choir tables, flower stands, and music stands, and some choreography is simply not possible within some *sanctuary* spaces. An on-site visit is very helpful for a walk-through of the space. Knowledge of the space also informs the choreographer to know how many dancers to use, as well as their age, ability, and costume requirements.

3. With regard to using live music, the troupe director must receive a copy of the sheet music and a recording of the music as it will be played within the worship service.

4. Choreograph the dances to be performed. This often takes weeks or sometimes months to create, depending on the amount of material requested by the church.

5. Teach the dance to the dancers. This may take several weeks or longer.

6. Rehearse the dancers until the dances are ready to share in worship. Rehearsals may take several weeks or months prior to the event because the choreographer is working with movement, music, timing, focus, space, and unity of a dance ensemble.

7. On-site rehearsal in the sanctuary where the dance(s) will be performed. This is very important and the dancers need to have a spacing rehearsal without the musicians or readers

PART III—Practical Areas Regarding Liturgical Dance

first. Be prepared for spontaneous "unknowns" in spacing rehearsals that will occur even if the dancers have previously seen the space in a photograph or had the privilege of an on-site visit. Often repertory dances must be re-choreographed to adapt to spatial problems such as sacrament celebration additions, church season additions, or additional people assisting in worship.

As you can see, this is a ministry that requires a great deal of time, not only due to creation and analysis of the choreography, but also rehearsals, and certainly unique spatial issues that sanctuaries innately have within their structure. The following is the fee scale used by Moving Liturgy Dance Ensemble which may be a helpful guide for other liturgical dance groups. This fee scale is flexible based on church size and the complexity of the requested material.

Fee Scale for Moving Liturgy Dance Ensemble

(Fees are set, but negotiable within reason and circumstance)

$75—*Choreographic fee for each new choreographed work* not currently in repertory. This does not pertain to works of multiple sections such as cantatas or medleys, but rather single hymns, prayers, or processionals. If work is in repertory, only a rehearsal/performance fee is charged.

$75—*Rehearsal/Performance fee per dancer for two dances shared in worship.* If dance is already in repertory, this is the fee for two dances. There is no fee charged for performance of spoken *Lord's Prayer*. However, there is a fee charged for instrumental/sung version. For only one dance of worship shared, fee is $50/dancer.

$400—*Liturgical Dance Workshop for group gathering.* This is a full three-hour workshop of liturgical dance information including history and background, learning movements and vocabulary,

Fees: To Charge or Not To Charge?

prayers, processionals, scripture passages, and hymns. Two or three members of the company usually accompany the workshop leader, often demonstrating and teaching repertory. The workshop usually occurs on a Saturday morning from nine to twelve AM, or Saturday or Sunday afternoon from two to five PM.

$150—*One hour Lecture Demonstration by Jane Wellford*

$600—*Full 1-Hour Worship Concert of Liturgical Dance Repertory Works with full company.* This often takes place on a Saturday night or Sunday afternoon or evening in the church sanctuary or fellowship hall. Rehearsal/performance fee is included in this fee.

$250—*Choreographic fee for newly commissioned work of five or more sections* such as cantatas, special anthems of multiple sections, seasonal works with sections, etc.

$400—*Performance/rehearsal fee for entire troupe as a whole for new commissioned work* such as a cantata, requiem, or other such work of five or more sections.

$1500—*Full Weekend Residency*—Saturday morning three-hour workshop, Saturday evening or Sunday afternoon one-hour worship concert, Sunday morning dances shared within liturgy. An additional fee of $50 is charged if church has more than one morning service and dances are repeated as long as material is same.

In addition to these expenses, travel, lodging, and food expenses are to be paid by the host group if dancers stay overnight. For same-day visits, the troupe will usually travel in one van for locations of five or fewer hours, and charge only for actual gas put in our tank, not cents per mile. If the worship service is held within a two to three-hour driving distance, the troupe will usually return home that evening and does not stay overnight. If overnight stay is required, the host group will provide food/lodging expenses, often two hotel rooms, or host site homes for the group of five or six dancers.

CHAPTER 12

How to Create a Liturgical Dance Group for Your Church

MUCH LIKE PLANTING A garden begins with good seeds, proper soil, and the right garden tools, starting a liturgical dance group needs to be handled in a step-by-step manner for a positive outcome. As mentioned in *Chapter 5: The Director or Choreographer of the Liturgical Dance Group*, it is important to begin the group with someone knowledgeable in the field of liturgical dance who also understands the faith in which she is participating as the group's director. Communication with church leaders and a worship committee is always wise prior to starting any new ministry within a church. Once the seed is planted, it is recommended to have ongoing dialogue between the liturgical dance director and the church's worship committee regarding liturgical dance within the church. Goals and objectives need to be shared and given a green light by clergy and/or worship committee prior to getting started. Once approved, proceed with enthusiasm in forming a liturgical dance group and embarking upon this beautiful worship art in your church.

How to Create a Liturgical Dance Group for Your Church

Suggested Steps *Prior to* Creating the Dance Group

1. Have a church family night supper where liturgical dance is introduced as the program after the evening meal. This may be presented by an outside group with quality liturgical dance examples shown, followed by a sharing of history and background information on liturgical dance. Included within the program would be some information about the history of liturgical dance in Christian worship. where a few examples are shared such as prayers, processionals, or scripture passages.

2. Have one or two dances shared within your church's worship service by an outside liturgical dance group of quality so the congregation may see what liturgical dance is like and its possibilities for enriching the liturgy. Preview this group ahead of time to make sure this is the group you want to bring in since there are many styles of liturgical dance. Make sure it is the right fit and style of liturgical dance for *your* church. Within the worship service, have a bulletin insert explaining the definition and purpose of liturgical dance. This is important in laying the foundation to assist your congregation's understanding.

3. Have a liturgical dance workshop at your church on a Saturday or a Sunday led by a competent liturgical dance specialist. Extend the invitation to the members of your church as well as the community who are interested in learning about liturgical dance. This is a great way to identify interest and possible membership for your group. Give a special invitation to your church worship committee so they can become educated about this potential worship art for your church. Make sure to register all attendees and ask them to leave their personal contact information so that you may have this on file.

PART III—Practical Areas Regarding Liturgical Dance

United in Prayer, Sam Eisenstadt, Fiona Koch, Matthew Baker, Leigh Stanfill, Heather Zachary, Kaelyn Green, Miles Williams, Katelyn Smith, photo by Kim Baker.

4. Once interest is established and you have the names of those who attended the initial workshop, proceed with setting up an interest meeting and possible first rehearsal. Even if it begins with only three or four interested members from your church and community, it is a start, and it will continue to grow.

5. Auditions are an option for the liturgical dance director, but you may want to think twice about this. It could become potentially awkward since this is a church ministry as well as an encouraged all-inclusive worship art. All those desiring to participate should feel welcomed, and it is up to a gifted ensemble director to rehearse and have all participants work well together. The more skilled dancers in the group could have leadership roles and advanced opportunities. The group's director may or may not participate as either a choreographer or a dancer. The director may choose to bring in an outside choreographer for the group. Some of the dancers may even create their own group dances from some of the suggestions below.

Once Established, Begin!

1. At the first meeting, share a collective prayer to ask God's presence and blessing on what you are about to do as a ministry within worship. Pray for focus and creativity as you begin.

2. Make sure everyone understands this is a *liturgical dance* group. Stress the intention of liturgical dance within worship (*Chapter 3: Intention of Liturgical Dance*). Share background history of dance in Christian worship (*Chapter 1: What is Liturgical Dance?*) and go over some basic movement vocabulary for liturgical dance such as terms. See *Part V, Glossary I: Terms for Liturgical Dance*. Share and teach posturing, dance technique, and focused presence as early as the beginning week and repeat this regularly.

Sharing and Blessing, Heather Zachary and Katelyn Smith, photo by Kim Walker.

3. Find out the experience level and personal interest of each member in the group. You may discover there are experienced dancers and choreographers within this group. Ask about their worship experiences and where they would like

PART III—Practical Areas Regarding Liturgical Dance

to see the worship proceed through their investment of dance in worship.

4. Have participants come to their first liturgical dance class wearing something comfortable, such as dancewear or exercise clothing. Begin with simple stretching to music followed by a simple modern or contemporary dance warm-up. Possible choices for music might be classical, world or ethnic, drums, contemporary, or whatever the group feels comfortable using.

5. The director may teach the group a processional hymn with simple steps for the current church season such as Palm Sunday, Advent, or Lent. Perhaps use palm branches for Palm Sunday and carry candles for Lent and Advent. For helpful examples, See *Chapter 13: Choreography for Liturgical Dance*.

6. Ask the choir director, minister, organist or worship committee leader what music or scriptures they would like to have brought to life through movement within the church lectionary readings or church seasonal music.

7. Have dancers bring in their favorite Christian music and brainstorm ideas and work in groups (stanza by stanza) until ideas start to form into beautiful creations for potential worship sharing. This may lead to the liturgical dance group choosing their own dance they would like to offer within worship. It is a good idea to check with the minister, organist, or choir director to see if and when the dance could most appropriately be shared. If music will be used, check whether or not it would be live with your church's choir members and organist, or pre-recorded. As director of the group, oversee any final dances making sure they are well-rehearsed and ready to share with the congregation.

8. When choreographing with texts from hymns, scripture, prayers, litanies, or poems, try to use only key words in a line, perhaps abstracting the essence of their meaning, not miming the words. Interpreting too many words per line only "muddies the water" and often confuses those receiving the

dance. Clarity and simplicity of movement are important to those viewing. The intention is to enhance, not to frustrate the viewers.

Filled with Great Joy, Miles Williams, photo by Kim Walker.

9. During rehearsals, continue to work on posturing and presence while working on the physical embodiment of the shared words and music the dancers will learn. Discuss Bible stories, parables, psalms, hymns, and simple prayers as possibilities to embody action words and scenarios. Entire stories from sacred texts and other sources are also great possibilities. Have the group bring their Bibles from home or use hymnals

PART III—Practical Areas Regarding Liturgical Dance

from the church sanctuary to get started. Each class could be a study of a different hymn or scriptural text. Consider asking the entire group to write a collective litany or prayer to be danced in worship on a given Sunday.

10. Focus when rehearsing and sharing is extremely important to stress. The dancer sharing liturgical dance in front of a congregation should give clear focus of body and face to each movement. This gives the intended movements more integrity. If the dancer doesn't show serious intent and focus while dancing, the congregation is certainly not going to believe or understand the dance she is sharing. When unison movements are choreographed, whether simple or complex, the dancers should be well rehearsed for clear understanding so that the dance does not look confusing.

11. Dress appropriately when sharing dances in worship. What the dancers wear speaks volumes even before the movements have begun. It is also important not to put dancers in attire that makes *them* feel uncomfortable or awkward. Color choices are important since color carries strong symbolic connotations and triggers responses from those viewing. It is important for the group director to be informed of the church seasons and the colors the seasons represent. Many church members know the church seasons and are aware of their colors and symbolic significance. Church seasonal colors are noted in *Chapter 10: Costume Suggestions*. Possible costumes might include:

> *Biblical or period costumes* (borrow from your Christmas pageant stock!)
>
> *Choir robes* or chasuble *robes*
>
> *Black pants and black or white tops.*
>
> *Blue jeans and white t-shirts* (youth groups do this often)

How to Create a Liturgical Dance Group for Your Church

Order costumes online or from local dance studio catalogues from the *Worship Dance, Praise Dance, or Lyrical Dance* section.

Being a part of a liturgical dance ensemble is not "second class" dancing. On the contrary, it should be strong and inspirational. The members of the ensemble should be willing to work together to become "enhancers of the word" through their movements. Some may have to work harder than others, but it is the responsibility of the ensemble director to rehearse everyone well for their participation in worship. It is a disservice to the dancers and the congregation for the ensemble to look unprepared, vague, or confused when sharing before the worshipping community. Once the group is well rehearsed, everyone should feel confident about the shared experience in worship.

The main point to remember is that a liturgical dance ensemble is much more than creating and rehearsing dances for worship. It is a way to have deep Christian fellowship while having the opportunity for analysis and study of the scriptures and music. The opportunity to enrich one's personal faith journey and enhance the corporate worship of the congregation can be extremely fulfilling. The creativity and rehearsal components of the dances are certainly a large part of the experience. When the time arrives for sharing the created dances where the dancers are truly worshipping as they dance, then it is truly a meaningful and powerful ministry for all participants and recipients to enjoy.

CHAPTER 13

Choreography for Liturgical Dance

As a choreographer and performer of liturgical dance, I feel my most spiritual and reverent connection with God within the creative process. Through analysis, research, creating the form and structure, and ultimately sharing liturgical dance, I am in worship. Throughout my youth, attending church on Sundays and being exposed to beautiful hymns, anthems, and texts made an indelible impression on me. I was just waiting to grow and mature into the choreographer I was to become and combine my love of sacred music and text embodied with movement.

Within this chapter, I will share a variety of dances I have choreographed for worship, from simple to complex. Some terms for dance, choreography, and church architecture referenced within the dances will be in italics. The italicized words may or may not be familiar to the reader and may be found in *Part V, Glossaries of Terms* in the end of this book for easy reference.

At this writing, I have choreographed over 237 dances of worship. My choreography includes prayers, processionals, calls to worship, benedictions, parables, hymns, anthems, cantatas, litanies, requiems, scripture readings, traditional and contemporary poems, dance dramas with spoken and danced texts, and sermons. I am particularly grateful to my earliest inspiration from the writings of Margaret Fisk Taylor Doane where my hunger to learn about liturgical dance was first introduced.

Choreography for Liturgical Dance

Prayers, Songs, Parables, and Processionals for Liturgical Dance

The Lord's Prayer

The Holy Bible, NIV, Matthew 6:9–13

May be performed anytime, anywhere by a
soloist or entire group of dancers
Elementary level: Children—Adults

Our Father

> Lunge forward with bent right leg. Right leg is rotated open to the right from the hip, but in front of body with right foot turned out to right. Left leg stays in place with heel on floor and foot turned outward to left. Hands are in prayer position. Elbows are lifted to make arms appear parallel to floor, and head is bowed.

Who art in heaven

> Remain in same pose as above.

Hallowed be thy name

> Lift both arms straight up parallel above head level, then reach them outward and over towards congregation with palms facing upward as you lunge forward into a deep, low bow, with arms ending down by sides at hips, fingers near floor. Head and neck are in line with back, focus is down.

Thy kingdom come

> Bring right foot back together beside left foot and stand erect facing front. Left arm returns down by left side, right arm reaches straight up making a fist with hand, as eyes and face focus looking upward at fist.

PART III—Practical Areas Regarding Liturgical Dance

Thy will be done

> Feet stay the same, right arm stays up; left arm extended out front, with bent elbow placing forearm about twelve inches away in front of chest, palm is flat and facing down. Then left arm extends stretching outward toward congregation as if smoothing over a table cloth, until it stops to left. Eye focus follows left arm as it moves to left. Both arms are now forming a right angle.

On earth as it is in heaven

> Step out to right on right foot about eighteen inches into a wide *plié* (deep knee bend) as you bring both arms parallel down left, sweeping them low towards floor as you continue to bring them up high to the right into the shape of a double open scythe pose. This position is made with each arm in an elongated scoop upward with palms facing up, left arm in front and lower than right arm. As you make this shape, shift standing weight onto right leg while left leg is pointed out to left side, eyes focused above scythe pose. (Option of stance with weight shift: Step into a *relevé* open *fourth position* on both feet, with same focus.)

Give us this day our daily bread

> Face left, shifting weight onto left leg, going down on right knee facing left, reaching both arms out to left with right hand resting on left hand, with both palms flat and open, as if to receive communion. Focus is slightly upward to the left, well above hands.

And forgive us our trespasses as we forgive those who trespass against us

> Stand up with weight on left foot, make a quarter turn left to face back away from congregation, clasp both hands and stretch arms up above head while you look upward, to ceiling as if pleading to God. Head is slightly back to give room for stretched arms.

Choreography for Liturgical Dance

Lead us not into temptation

> Pivot one-half turn right to face congregation. Kneeling down on left knee with both arms bent at elbows in front of face, forearms in front of you parallel to floor, palms facing toward congregation, right arm in front of eyes, left arm in front of chin; arms are hiding face but not touching face, finger length of one arm is even with elbows of other arm. This position looks like you are blocking something from coming at you.

But deliver us from evil

> Still on left knee, extend right leg straight out to right diagonal. Clasp hands and extend both arms out over right leg on same diagonal, parallel to floor, while arching upper back and looking upward to ceiling. Head and arms should pull in opposite directions.

For Thine is the kingdom

> Stand up and turn one-half turn to right with your back to congregation, placing both feet together, toes slightly turned out. Lift right arm upward, keeping it straight from beginning of reach to end of reach, into a high diagonal to right side with focus on right hand. Left arm is still down by left side.

And the power and the glory

> Stay same pose, but add left arm reach upward to match the right arm to complete a "V" shape with arms. Focus is now upward to left hand on words "power and the glory."

Forever and ever

> Do two and one-half *pump turns* or *paddle turns* to right with arms remaining in a "V" while looking upward, balcony height. End turns facing congregation in front. Dancer may walk in a circle if turning is too challenging.

PART III—Practical Areas Regarding Liturgical Dance

Amen.

> Lunge forward on right leg in prayer position with arms in front, hands together, head bowed, just like in beginning pose with elbows lifted parallel to floor.

Hands

Prayer by Charles M. Olsen[1]

Elementary level: Children—Adults

The narrator of this prayer will stand outside the circle to read for the participants. She will ask participants to gather in a circle standing, close their eyes, and make tight fists with their hands by their sides. Prior to beginning the prayer, the narrator asks everyone to listen to the words of the prayer and move their hands according to the simple verbal cues within the prayer such as "lift them up to you" or "reach out to clasp the hand." Prior to beginning the prayer, the narrator might suggest that participants lift up their joined hands at the end of the prayer on the verbal cue "shape us together into the body of Christ. Amen."

Let us pray . . .

> I see, Lord, in *my tightly clenched fists,* the representation of myself,
>
> My cares, possessions, pride.
>
> I shut you out, lest you change me.
>
> I shut other people out, lest they would know me, lest they would hurt me.
>
> In fact, I could strike out with these fists against those who would threaten me.

---

1. Olsen, *Hands, Presbyterian Survey,* 1969, Volume 59, 15.

Choreography for Liturgical Dance

Guided by the Star, Leigh Stanfill, Katelyn Smith, Fiona Koch, photo by Kim Walker.

But I see in the whitened knuckles and tense forearms what this is doing to me.

I am up-tight, enslaved, imprisoned within myself.

I am tired, tense, lonely, and am only destroying myself.

And now, in *slowly opening my hands*,

I release myself to you, Lord.

Take my guilt, burdens, cares, emptiness, and loneliness.

My arms no longer hurt. My knuckles are no longer white.

PART III—Practical Areas Regarding Liturgical Dance

Thank you for release, for freedom, for peace.

With *open hands*, I can no longer shut you out;

Shut out other people, or strike out against those who would threaten me.

Open hands are for helping.

Fill them with your love, show them what to do.

How to witness, how to serve.

Suddenly I am aware of the hurts and needs of other persons and other situations.

In my mind's eye, I place them in these hands and *lift them up to you* for your sustaining grace and healing touch.

No longer alone, I *reach out to clasp the hand* of my sister and brother.

I thank you for them, I pray for them.

Shape us together into the body of Christ. Amen.

Parable of the Sower

The Holy Bible, NIV, Mark 4:3-8, 14-20

A combination of dance and pedestrian movements
with non-speaking movement roles
One narrator needed as storyteller.
Elementary—Intermediate Level: Children—Adults

Requirements: One narrator and four small groups. *Group 4* may start with very few dancers, and will have dancers added during the story. Additional dancers to *Group 4* will have a small extra role in the beginning of the parable; one as *farmer*, one as *bird*, one as *sun*, and the *Group 1* of seeds that rolled away. All of these characters may join *Group 4* (Good seeds group) after they have all crossed the stage, getting into their second roles from the back

Choreography for Liturgical Dance

of the groups. The narrator may be any adult or youth member of the church or worship community with a good speaking voice. The narrator stands off to the side and reads the parable for those participating. The groups may be as large or as small as needed. The beginning of the play starts with all participants on stage standing with their assigned group, facing back when the narrator begins speaking. *Farmer*, *Bird*, and *Sun* are off to side of *chancel*. Within the direction of this parable, I will use the word "stage" rather than *chancel*. Stage direction terms are found in *See Glossary A for Spatial Directions for staging*.

Four groups of seeds:

> *Group 1*: Seeds birds ate and/or seeds that rolled away as if windblown.
>
> *Group 2*: Seeds that grew too fast, were scorched by the sun, and withered.
>
> *Group 3*: Seeds that grew up with thorns and were choked by thorns.
>
> *Group 4*: Seeds that grew and flourished. Good seeds.

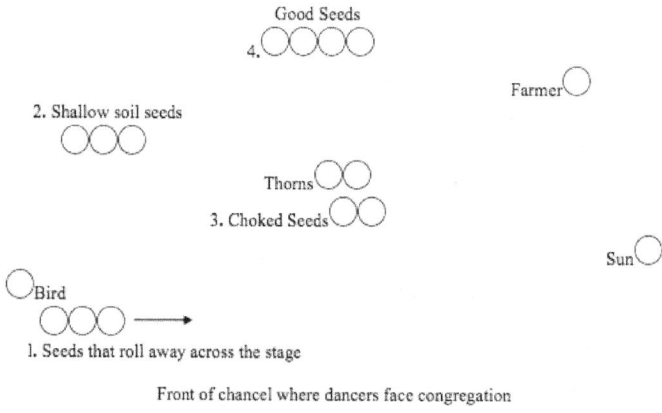

PART III—Practical Areas Regarding Liturgical Dance

Narrator: "Listen! A farmer went out to sow his seed."

Farmer: Walks or dances across stage (from *downstage left* towards *downstage right*) as if scattering seeds from a seed pouch. *Farmer* makes sure he throws seeds in the directions of each group. *Farmer* then completes crossing of stage to other side and quietly and unnoticed, joins in back of *Group 4* at the end of his crossing.

All Seed Groups: Slowly turn right, face front, and go down into a low squat like little seeds, heads bowed down, as if not seen. Dancers are now seeds under the soil!

Narrator: "As he was scattering the seed, some fell along the path, and the birds came and ate it up."

Group 1: (Bird and Seeds that rolled away) Seeds blown away or eaten begin rolling in a group of tight little balls from *stage right* across to *stage left* and are chased across stage by the bird right behind them, dancing and flying and trying to peck at them on their travel across the stage. Seeds of *Group 1* all make it across stage. Quietly and unnoticed after crossing, all seeds in this group, and the bird, stand up and walk quietly and unnoticed to join *Group 4*, the "good seeds group."

Narrator will pause briefly and allow movement to occur prior to reading next line.

Narrator: "Some seed fell on rocky places, where there was not much soil. It sprang up quickly, because the soil was shallow. But when the sun came up, the plants were scorched, and withered because they had no root."

Group Two: (Shallow Soil Seeds & Sun) *Shallow soil seeds* do a slow moving upward growth process to a standing position, with sprouts sticking out to sides as if wheat stalks in any shapes they choose. This might look somewhat like a flower or other type plant blooming in slow motion like time lapsed photography. The end product should look somewhat like a wheat stalk full grown. It is great for each dancer to look uniquely different at full growth. The *Sun* enters from *stage left* on the reader's line "when the sun came up" and dances gracefully across the stage with widespread arms beaming out like sun beams, and continues to travel over to the opposite side of stage to *stage right*. Right after the sun passes, all *Group 2* seeds that just grew all the way up begin to slowly wither and die because they are scorched by the sun and slowly descend to the ground and end in any low level pose on or near the ground they desire.

Narrator: "Other seed fell among thorns, which grew up and choked the plants, so that they did not bear grain."

Group 3: (Choked Seeds & Thorns) All seeds and thorns in this group grow slowly upward together, using any desired shape they choose as their final outcome. At the end of their growth, the *thorns*, who are standing behind the *seeds to be choked,* slowly lift their thorns (arms) high above the seeds who are now plants in front of them, and choke them around the neck (dramatized, not real) and cause the plants in front to slowly collapse to floor. It is of good humor for the plants in front of the thorns to show expression on their faces as if in pain from the thorns and for the thorns to look large and powerful. The choked plants remain on the floor in low level or "fainted" poses while the thorns remain on one knee above the plants in some form or shape after the chocking as if they are tougher.

Awe and Majesty, Anita Davis, Jane Wellford, Ingrid Murphy, Ginger Strickland, Betsy Reeves, photo by Debbie Lynch.

PART III—Practical Areas Regarding Liturgical Dance

Narrator: "Still other seeds fell on good soil. It came up, grew and produced a crop, multiplying thirty, sixty, or even a hundred times."

Group 4 (Good Seeds): The *good seeds* now slowly grow up into whatever plant shapes they would like to become. They look fabulous, happy, and wonderful because they have a good life and have "made it." They may even dance around in a circle, being mindful they have a plant shape to keep as they dance, but may move their leaves or stalks as if showing off their "good seed status." The choreographer has the liberty to give them anything to do here, unison or individual movements, depending on their abilities.

Narrator: "He who has ears to hear let him hear."

All groups freeze in their final pose with energy.

After the parable is told the first time, *all groups* (including the Bird, the Sun, the Farmer, and Group 1 Rolling Seeds) go and stand in their original spaces, all facing back, until they are spoken about in the final parable explanation. The parable's meaning will now be read again by the *Narrator* from Mark 4:14-20. Before *Narrator* reads, all groups turn and face front, and go down again as seeds. As each character or group is mentioned, they simply do their parts again as the *Narrator* explains the meaning.

Narrator: "The *Farmer* sows the Word. Some people are like the seed along the path, where the Word is sown," like *Group 1*. "As soon as they hear it, Satan," the *Bird*, "comes and takes away the Word that was sown in them. Others," like *Group 2 and the Sun*, who are "the seed sown on rocky places, hear the Word and at once receive it with joy. But since they have no root, they last only a short time. When trouble or persecution comes because of the Word, they quickly fall away. Still others," like *Group 3*, the seed sown among thorns, "hear the Word; but the worries of this life, the deceitfulness of wealth and the desires for other things come in and choke the Word, making it unfruitful. Others," like Group 4, the seed sown on good soil, "hear the Word, accept it, and produce a crop thirty, sixty or even a hundred times what was sown."

Depending on the ability and age level of dance and drama within the group, this parable has multiple options as to how it may be performed. From young children in a simplified version, to adults in a more complex version, this danced parable is usually always a success.

Father, I Adore You

Music and Lyrics by Terrye Coelho

Copyright © 1972 Cccm Music (ASCAP) Universal Music—Brentwood Benson Publishing (ASCAP) (adm. at CapitalCMG-Publishing.com) All rights reserved. Used by permission.
Beginning Level: Youth—Adults
A commitment song with only three repeating movements.

Music and movements in this version will be used in a canon after learning in unison. Participants initially begin standing in a single circle with hands by sides to learn movements. The song later progresses into three concentric circles for final version of all three verses in canon with movements.

Stanza 1
Father, I adore You

> Hands in prayer position, hands flat together, elbows lifted parallel to floor

Lay my life before You

> Slowly, bring arms down to sides with palms open facing center of circle

PART III—Practical Areas Regarding Liturgical Dance

How I love You

> Slowly, lift arms upward to shoulder height, palms facing up, slightly outward from front of self, but not in front of person beside you.

Stanza 2
Jesus, I adore You

> Repeat same gestures as line one, *Stanza 1*

Lay my life before You

> Repeat same gestures as line two, *Stanza 1*

How I love You

> Repeat same gestures as line three, *Stanza 1*)

Stanza 3
Spirit, I adore You

> Repeat same gestures as line one, *Stanza 1*

Lay my life before You

> Repeat same gestures as line two, *Stanza 1*

How I love You

> Repeat same gestures as line three, *Stanza 1*

Directions for Canon: After everyone has learned the song and sung all three stanzas through in one circle in unison, then the song is to be sung and performed in a canon in three concentric circles with singing and movements together.

Center circle (needs at least three to four people): This first group of the canon who is the center circle begins singing with movements of line one, *Stanza 1*, and does not stop singing with movements, continuing through entire song, all three stanzas.

Choreography for Liturgical Dance

Middle circle (needs five or more people): After the center circle sings line one, *Stanza 1*, the middle circle, the second group, begins singing line one, *Stanza 1*, and continues through all three stanzas with singing and movements.

Outside circle (at least six or more people): After the middle circle sings line one, *Stanza 1*, the outside circle, the third group, begins line one, *Stanza 1*, with singing and movements, continuing through all three stanzas.

All three stanzas of this song are to be sung in this canon style of singing, complete with the movements until the outside circle has completed all three stanzas. By the end of singing all three stanzas in canon, the aerial view of this movement song looks like a flower opening and closing, in full bloom by the end of the song, with everyone's arms lifted with palms open. Each circle is to hold their final movements until all three circles have completed their singing. It is a good idea to put at least one strong singer in each circle, and two strong singers in the center circle as leaders.

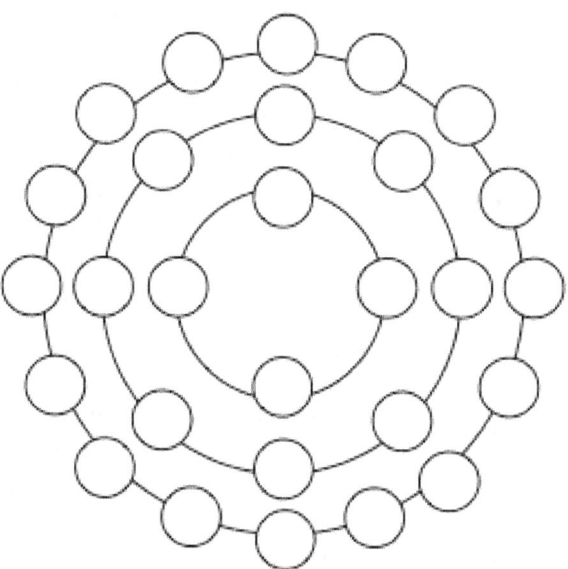

part iii—Practical Areas Regarding Liturgical Dance

Amazing Grace

Lyrics by John Newton, American Melody

A hymn for any church season representing grace, mercy and forgiveness. This hymn is found in most hymnbooks and is sometimes four or five stanzas in length.
Intermediate—Advanced Level: Youth—Adults

This is a favorite hymn at worship services, small group gatherings, and certainly liturgical dance workshops. The multi-sensory group sharing of this hymn with movement often conveys an emotional, visual, and auditory tapestry that is powerful.

The leader should bring each stanza of this four or five stanza hymn printed in large text on separate notecards. Make a circle of everyone participating. Have people number off one to four if four stanzas, or one to five if five stanzas. Each of the four or five groups is given one card with a stanza of *Amazing Grace*. Ask the groups to move to separate spaces throughout the room. Each group designates one member of the group to read the stanza on the card aloud to their group as the group listens to the words. Have each group *stand* in their own small circle to discuss what the words to their particular stanza mean to them, allowing each person in the group to comment. If they sit, it is more difficult for them to think of active movements to share. Keep them standing. Have each group collaboratively create a few visual movement images of their stanza to the words on the card they are given. This can be a simple movement phrase of two to three movements (pedestrian or stylized) per line, or a more complex and complete dance of the stanza. The choreography is completely dependent upon the age and ability of those participating.

Allow about fifteen minutes to create and practice, then have each group return to one large circle. Have a recording of the sung version of *Amazing Grace* you want to accompany the choreography for the group and allow them to hear the melody and tempo before the song is shared with movement together. Inform the group they will share the hymn in one large circle with each group

Choreography for Liturgical Dance

stepping into the center as they perform their stanza. The instructor must determine where front will be in the circle. After each group's stanza is shared, they will slowly step back into place into the greater circle. This will continue until all stanzas are shared. Start the music and begin. After the hymn is shared, ask which physical images remained in the participants' minds from this familiar hymn as it was danced. This causes a deeper reflection due to the multi-sensory experience of words, music, and movement. Have participants repeat the hymn with movements a second time, and you will be amazed how beautiful it has become after it is discussed and performed a second time. Suggest any suggested changes if necessary.

If you like the results, ask your minister if those present at this rehearsal could share this in an upcoming Sunday worship experience. It should be presented in the *chancel* where your circle will now become a semi-circle open to the front so those present in the congregation may see the story clearly revealed. It would work best if you have a member of the congregation sing *Amazing Grace* a cappella, or sing the words with musical accompaniment. This works best when the congregation does not have to sing the hymn as the dancers dance since the congregation may miss the interpretation through the movements while looking down at the words in their hymnals.

They'll Know We Are Christians

Lyrics and music by Peter Scholtes

© 1993 Lorenz Publishing Co.
All Rights Reserved. International Copyright Secured.
Permission granted by the Lorenz Corporation
Beginning Level: Children—Adults

This hymn is set to simple movements for all ages. It is danced in a circle while holding hands, perhaps after a family night supper

PART III—Practical Areas Regarding Liturgical Dance

or other church gathering. It is well suited for use of the traveling *tripudium step*, three steps forward and one step back. See further explanation for this step in *Part V, Glossary I: Terms for Liturgical Dance*.

Stanza 1
We are one in the Spirit, we are one in the Lord.
We are one in the Spirit, we are one in the Lord.
And we pray that all unity may one day be restored.

> All join hands and travel to *right* doing the *tripudium step* six times. Begin *tripudium* step on right foot when traveling right, taking three steps forward (right, left, right) followed by one step back on the left foot. Repeat 5 more times.

Refrain: And they'll know we are Christians by our love, by our love, Yes, they'll know we are Christians by our love

> Take eight regular walking steps to center of circle holding hands as you lift arms up.
>
> Take eight regular walking steps back to place bringing arms down.

Stanza 2
We will walk with each other, we will walk hand in hand.
We will walk with each other, we will walk hand in hand.
And together we'll spread the news that God is in our land.

> *Tripudium step* begins to *left* on left foot repeated six times, back step on right foot.

Refrain: And they'll know we are Christians by our love, by our love, Yes, they'll know we are Christians by our love

> Take eight regular walking steps to center of circle holding hands as you lift arms up.
>
> Take eight regular walking steps back to place bringing arms down

Choreography for Liturgical Dance

Stanza 3
We will work with each other, we will work side by side.
We will work with each other, we will work side by side.
And we'll guard each one's dignity, and save each one's pride.

> *Tripudium step* begins to *right* on right foot repeated six times, back step on left foot

Refrain: And they'll know we are Christians by our love, by our love, Yes, they'll know we are Christians by our love.

> Take eight regular walking steps to center of circle holding hands as you lift arms up.

> Take eight regular walking steps back to place bringing arms down.

Stanza 4
All praise to the Father, from whom all things come.
And all praise to Christ Jesus, His only Son.
And all praise to the Spirit, who makes us one.

> *Tripudium step* begins to *left* on left foot repeated six times, back step on right foot.

Refrain: And they'll know we are Christians by our love, by our love, Yes, they'll know we are Christians by our love

> Take eight regular walking steps to center of circle holding hands as you lift arms up.

> Take eight regular walking steps back to place bringing arms down.

Processional Dances Using Tripudium Step

There are many occasions to use the wonderful *tripudium step* in processional dances. I have chosen to use this early Christian processional step on numerous occasions due to its simplicity and its historic significance. After *O Come, O Come, Emmanuel*, see a

PART III—Practical Areas Regarding Liturgical Dance

listing for many Christian seasonal hymns for use of this meaningful historic processional step.

O Come, O Come, Emmanuel

Written by John Mason Neale, Phillip Kristianson, and Thomas Helmore

Copyright © 2005 Universal Music—Brentwood Benson Publishers (ASCAP) (adm.at CapitalCMGPublishing.com) All rights reserved. Used by permission
An Advent hymn to celebrate the coming of Christ
Intermediate—Advanced Level: Youth—Adults

Three to five dancers suggested for this version. Dancers may carry real or electric candles coming down the *aisle(s)* in this *processional* dance. Dancers enter the *sanctuary* from the *narthex*, traveling either single or double file, dancing the *tripudium step*. It is nice to have *sanctuary* lights slightly dimmed and have this hymn open an evening or daytime Advent service of worship.

Stanza 1
O Come, O Come, Emmanuel,

> Beginning on right foot, take two *tripudium steps* at a slow, even pace.

And ransom captive Israel,

> Repeat movements for first line choreography

That mourns in lonely exile here,

> Repeat movements for first line choreography.

Until the Son of God appear,

> Dancers should be entering the *transept* and *chancel* areas by now, placing their candles either on the *altar, communion table,* or other flat area nearby as they go to their places in the *chancel* and *transept* doing two final

Choreography for Liturgical Dance

tripudium entry steps to get to their places before the refrain. Two dancers have stepped up into the chancel area by now, evenly spaced about thirty-six inches apart facing congregation, and three dancers should now be in the transept area facing the congregation with the two dancers behind them in the spaces between them. (see spacing figure below).

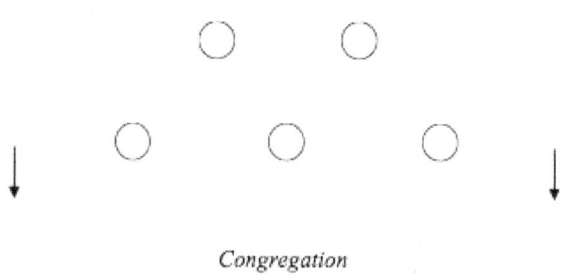

Congregation

Refrain: Rejoice! Rejoice!

On first "rejoice" all dancers do one *triplet turn* right traveling forward with arms open out to sides, palms facing up. On second "rejoice" dancers return back to places with one *triplet turn* left with same arms as first "rejoice" turn.

Emmanuel

Dancers lunge on right leg facing forward, bringing hands flat together into prayer position, elbows lifted with arms parallel to floor, head bowed.

Shall come to thee, O Israel!

On "*shall come to thee*," dancers step forward on left foot in front of right about seven inches apart with equal weight on both feet into a *relevé* (rising up on balls of feet), opening hands and lifting both arms up parallel about twelve inches apart with upward focus. On "O

PART III—Practical Areas Regarding Liturgical Dance

Israel," dancers lunge forward once again, this time on left foot by sliding right foot back, bringing both arms out toward congregation forward, then slowly down by sides almost to floor showing a deep reverent bow in a lunge, head focused down also.

Stanzas 2-4 and *Refrains*

Stanzas 2-4 may be choreographed and interpreted for soloists within the group, a different soloist, duet or trio for each stanza. Since *Stanza 1* is the processional entry, all dancers take part in *Stanza 1* with the *Refrain*. The *first soloist* would perform *Stanza 2* where words are interpreted for this verse. Following *Stanza 2, all dancers* join in to repeat the choreography for the *Refrain* together. A *second soloist* or a duet would perform *Stanza 3* where words are interpreted for this verse until the *Refrain* where all dancers again repeat the *Refrain* choreography together. Finally, a *third soloist* or a different duet or trio, performs *Stanza 4* where words are interpreted for this verse. After *Stanza 4*, all dancers once again, perform the final *Refrain* together, *or* a different ending such as celebrative traveling *triplet turn* circle alternating right and left turns until a final ending pose up in the chancel at the end of the final *Refrain*. While each soloist or duet is dancing, it is suggested that the other dancers turn to face away from the congregation after each *Refrain* to give attention to the soloist or duet who is sharing their own stanza. The dancers not dancing will usually be standing off to the sides in an equal number. On each *Refrain* where all dancers share in the dance, the choreography is always the same. Each of the four *stanzas* could easily lend itself to solos, duets or trios depending on ability of dancers.

Choreography for Liturgical Dance

Other Recommended Hymns for Using the Tripudium Step as a Processional Entry Dance

Theme	Hymn Title
Unity/World Peace	In Christ There Is No East or West
Worship/Adoration	Come Christians, Join and Sing
Loyalty/Courage	Onward Christian Soldiers
Communion	Let Us Break Bread Together
Lordship of Jesus	Fairest Lord Jesus
God's Hand in Nature	For the Beauty of the Earth
Worship/Adoration	Glorious Things of Thee Are Spoken
Worship/Adoration	Immortal, Invisible, God Only Wise
Fellowship with God	I Come to the Garden Alone
Worship/Adoration	Holy, Holy, Holy! Lord God Almighty
Confession/Repentance	Just As I Am, Without One Plea
God's Love	Love Divine, All Loves Excelling
Dedication/Devotion	Take Time to be Holy
Church/Reformation	The Church's One Foundation
Mission	We've a Story to Tell to the Nations
Thanksgiving	Rejoice, Ye Pure in Heart
Thanksgiving	We Gather Together
Thanksgiving	Come Ye Thankful People, Come

PART III—Practical Areas Regarding Liturgical Dance

Theme	Hymn Title
Advent	*Come Thou Long Expected Jesus*
Christmas	*It Came Upon the Midnight Clear*
Christmas	*O Come, All Ye Faithful*
Christmas	*Hark! The Herald Angels Sing*
Christmas	*O Little Town of Bethlehem*
Christmas	*We Three Kings of Orient Are*
Lent	*Were You There When They Crucified*
Lent	*O Sacred Head Now Wounded*
Lent	*Go to Dark Gethsemane*
Palm Sunday	*All Glory, Laud, and Honor*
Easter	*Crown Him with Many Crowns*
Easter	*Christ the Lord Is Risen Today*

Let the Words of My Mouth

Words and Music by Gail Loress Hamilton

Copyright © 1988 Warner-Tamerlane Publishing Corp. (BMI) and Loress Songs (BMI)
All Rights Administered by Warner-Tamerlane Publishing Corp.
All Rights Reserved. Used by permission of Alfred Music
This dance is a perfect Call to Worship or Benediction
Intermediate—Advanced Level: Youth—Adults

Choreography for Liturgical Dance

This dance begins with three dancers in the chancel on their knees facing outward in three different directions toward congregation, arms down by sides

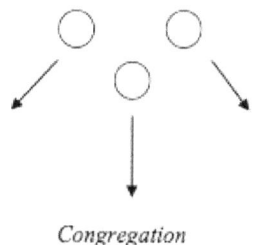

Congregation

Let the words of my mouth

>Dancers begin on knees with arms down by sides, facing outward with backs toward each other, about two feet apart. When music and words begin, dancers place both hands over their mouths, but not touching mouths, fingers of flat hands pointing toward each other, elbows lifted to make arms parallel with the floor.
>
>While still on knees, on "words," dancers extend arms outward to reveal "mouth" and the potential of speaking, palms are up, arms open fully at shoulder level, with dancers' focus outward.

Bring you praise

>Dancers arch back with three *windmill arms* (right, left, right, like backstroke) until third time arm movement touches floor, supporting dancer in a back arch while other arm is reaching straight upward, vertical toward ceiling with facial focus, following line of upward arm.
>
>Dancer in center may choose either arm for this movement, while side dancers must end with *downstage* arm down and *upstage* arm reaching up.

Let the words that I speak

>Dancers quickly stand and lunge on a bent leg outward from their same starting locations. Their hands are

PART III—Practical Areas Regarding Liturgical Dance

placed at their mouths as if they are shouting for a brief second as they begin the movement of their hands outward away from mouth in an outward, slightly upward diagonal to fully outstretched arms, focus in direction of head is facing.

All dancers do this simultaneously in their individual different diagonals on the word "speak."

Be seasoned with your love and grace

Dancers rise up into a *relevé* with right leg front, bringing back leg across front pivoting into a complete turn with arms lifting up from sides, palms facing outward as arms come up into *fifth position* over head. When arms are finally overhead, palms then face inward to where they are about five inches apart above head. Then lower hands and arms down in front of face and body, making quick back and forth movements with fingers only as if "sprinkling" seasoning down in front of body as hands are lowered all the way down to hang beside hips, as focus follows hands downward. Then all three dancers facing front, bring hands into prayer position and go into a lunge, center dancer closer to congregation than side dancers as in diagram. All prayer positions have elbows lifted to where they are parallel with the floor.

May the things, O Lord that I choose to say

All three dancers do a pivot turn toward the direction they will be going, run to change places with each other; side dancers change places with each other, while center dancer runs to back of triangle away from congregation *upstage*. At end of new location, each dancer lunges into a new pose *facing back* away from congregation towards cross or altar with hands up to mouth as if shouting gesture outwardly to God, then slowly bring their hands from their mouths to open out to the sides as if asking for God's guidance or a question gesture.

Bring glory, not shame, to your name each day

Each dancer pivots to run and face front (always in a triangle spacing) and takes two steps forward to jump

Choreography for Liturgical Dance

up on the word "glory," pushing off right foot, swinging arms up from sides to assist in the jump to full straight extension from shoulders. Then dancers quickly lower themselves down to floor on the word "shame," with left leg and arms catching body weight to assist in lying down on back quickly. (Less experienced dancers may choose to drop down into a low squat with arms down by sides.) On "name each day," dancers sit up and subtly move onto one knee by tucking left leg under body and reaching out with right arm over right knee on an upward diagonal as facial focus follows the reach.

Let the words of my mouth

Dancers gracefully get up from seated position by pushing off left foot and left hand onto right foot, continuing to reach with right arm to upward right diagonal as they take two steps forward right diagonal, keeping focus to uplifted right hand.

Bring you praise!

On "bring you" all dancers do three quick *pump turns* to the right with arms held high above head, about eighteen inches apart, in a more open *fifth position* with only slightly bent elbows, palms facing inward. On "praise," dancers step forward on right foot into an open *fourth position* into *relevé* (feet are about six-to eight inches apart and turned out with right foot front, left foot back) pressing both hands upward flat as if holding a large tray, with focus up and facing congregation.

Let them bring you praise!

Dancers gracefully do a little inhale lift pushing off front right foot as arms lift up in an over-arch above head from right to left. Dancers quickly walk around self to right and return to an ending pose in the center of chancel from where they began but in new positions. Center pose is as follows: *First dancer* is kneeling on floor on left knee facing upward right diagonal, torso is tilted slightly back with sternum and focus up to right with left arm in a large open curve reaching back behind body with palm

PART III—Practical Areas Regarding Liturgical Dance

up. Right arm is full length in front reaching forward with palm up looking in an upward right diagonal.

Second dancer stands in a lunge close behind first dancer who is kneeling and does the exact same pose with upper body, but lunging forward on right leg. *Third dancer* is just slightly behind second dancer doing a *fourth position relevé* on balls of feet with straight legs, with arms in same pose as first two dancers. All three have exact same facial focus and energy toward upward right diagonal. Hold this pose until music ends.

Joyful, Joyful, We Adore Thee

Lyrics by Henry van Dyke, music by Ludwig van Beethoven

Copyright © 1987 New Spring Publishing Inc. (ASCAP (adm.at CaitolCMGPublishing.com)
All rights reserved. Used by permission.
Intermediate/Advanced level: Youth—Adults

This is a four-stanza hymn in most hymnals, three-stanza in some hymnals, choreographed as a *processional* entry dance into the *sanctuary*. I have chosen to choreograph this dance for five dancers, but more or less dancers may be used depending on sanctuary space. Since flags are used in this choreography, please refer to *Chapter 10: Costumes for Liturgical Dance* regarding flags as props.

This dance is intended to be large, ceremonial, and joyful. Because this music is so grand, I have costumed the dancers in long dresses (or slacks and tunics) with chasuble robes over the top of dress or slacks. Each dancer would carry a pair of medium length liturgical flags as they dance. The entire first verse takes the dancers in a processional entry from the *narthex*, down the *aisle* (or *aisles*) into the *transept* and *chancel* area of the *sanctuary*.

Choreography for Liturgical Dance

Stanza 1
Joyful, Joyful, we adore Thee

>Beginning one at a time, allowing about five feet between each dancer, all dancers enter the *sanctuary* from the *narthex* down the center *aisle* doing the following step and carrying liturgical dance flags. (A) *Balancé* right (step right, left, right) sustain final counts with a slight suspended energy to right while swishing both flags over high to right using all musical counts; (B) Repeat *balancé* step to left (step left, right, left) sustain last counts to left with a slight suspended energy while swishing both flags over high to left taking entire musical counts; flags are held extremely high, with only slightly bent elbows.

God of glory, Lord of love

>(A) *Triplet-turn* right traveling forward on "God of glory" (right foot, left foot, right foot) holding both flags upward in a "V"

>(B) Still traveling forward on "*Lord of love*" do a *triplet step* forward (not a turn) beginning on left foot (left, right, left) as dancer scoops both flags in an under-scoop forward into a suspended "V" up high to front

Hearts unfold like flowers before Thee

>Repeat same steps from *line one* (A and B)

Opening to the sun above

>Repeat same steps from *line two* (A and B)

Melt the clouds of sin and sadness

>Repeat same steps from *line one* (A and B)

Drive the dark of doubt away

>Repeat same steps from *line two* (A and B)

Giver of immortal gladness

>Repeat same steps from *line one* (A and B)

part iii—Practical Areas Regarding Liturgical Dance

Fill us with the light of day

> Repeat same steps from *line two* (A and B). By end of *Stanza 1*, two dancers are up in *chancel* area, and three dancers are in *transept* area on a lower level, all dancers facing the congregation, equally spaced apart from one another. (See figure for spacing)

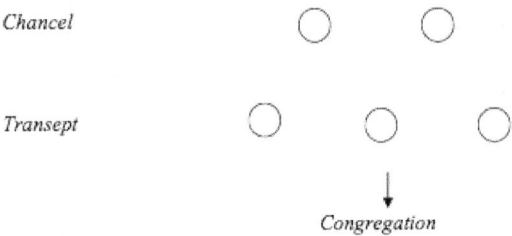

Stanza 2

(Dancing for *Stanzas 2, 3,* and *4* takes place in both the *transept* and the *chancel*)

All Thy works with joy surround Thee,

> Dancers are all facing congregation as in illustration at end of *Stanza 1*.
>
> *Balancé* to right side (right, left, right) with flags up high to right, sustain final count.
>
> *Balancé* to left side (left, right, left) with flags down medium level to left side, making a sweeping diagonal from up high right to down low left side, sustain final count

Choreography for Liturgical Dance

Earth and heaven reflect Thy rays,

> Windmill roll turn to right with flags at 180 degrees apart in a straight line as you take a three-step turn (right, left, right, sustain count four), then point left foot out to left side on count four. When feet stop, make an additional large circle with flags to left and have flags end up high to right side diagonal, with right flag twelve inches higher than left flag in two parallel lines, facial focus is up to flags.

Stars and angels sing around Thee

> Repeat movement from *Stanza 2, line one*, but reverse everything to the left side.

Center of unbroken praise

> Repeat movement from *Stanza 2, line two*, but reverse to left side.

Field and forest, vale and mountain

> Face front on slight right diagonal. On "*field*," jump up forward on right foot while scooping flags forward and up into a "V." On "*forest*," rock back on left foot while scooping flags back. Repeat same movements front and back in same order for "*vale*" and "*mountain*." (a jump forward on right, and rock back on left, two times)

Flowery meadow, flashing sea,

> Two *pump turns* right (these are eight quick repeated right down and left up steps while turning) making two revolutions, holding flags up in high "V"

Chanting bird and flowing fountain,

> Dancers face front on slight left diagonal. On "*chanting*," jump up forward on left foot while scooping flags forward and up into "V," then rocking back on "*bird*" on right foot; jumping up again on "*flowing*," and rocking back on right foot on "*fountain*" with same use of flags as *Stanza 2, line five*.

PART III—Practical Areas Regarding Liturgical Dance

Call us to rejoice in Thee

Repeat two *pump turns* to left as in *Stanza 2, line six*. End *Stanza 2* with all *transept dancers* running up into *chancel* area to join *chancel dancers* for next step as flags are held high on transition as dancers get into new positions. Last *pump turn* used for all dancers to get into place up in *chancel* for *Stanza 3*. One turn is cut out so dancers may travel to new positions. (See illustration below)

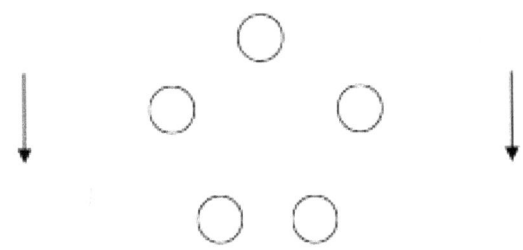

From chancel facing front toward congregation

Stanza 3
Thou art giving and forgiving,
Ever blessing, ever blest,

All dancers' right flags are held vertically in dancer's hands with a straight right arm out from shoulder touching each other's hands with extended arms in center of circle while left hand flags are held in a high diagonal to outside of circle. Dancers do four fairly quick *triplet* steps traveling clockwise direction in a circle beginning on left foot (left 2, 3, right 2, 3, left 2, 3, right 2, 3) with each direction and number being an actual step of the foot as steps alternate feet. Dancer should sustain count 3 a second longer on each count of the count 3's for all four triplet steps.

Choreography for Liturgical Dance

Wellspring of the joy of living,

> *Balancé* away from center of circle to outside left as you gracefully swish flags in a top arch toward outside of circle away from center (steps are left, right, left); then *balancé* inward toward center of circle swishing flags in a top arch over top toward center (steps are right, left, right).

Ocean depth of happy rest;

> Two *pump turns* left beginning on left foot (four down-ups for eight counts) toward outside of circle with flags held high in "V" ending facing opposite direction of pump turns, ready to begin *triplet* steps facing counter-clockwise beginning on right foot.

Thou our Father, Christ our Brother,
All who live in love are Thine;

> Repeat *Stanza 3, lines one* and *two*, using four *triplet steps* traveling in a counterclockwise direction beginning on right foot with *left flag to inside of circle* and *right flag to outside* of circle this time.

Teach us how to love each other,

> *Balancé* to right, away from center of circle, as you gracefully swish flags in a top arch to outside of circle away from center. Steps are right, left, right, sustain count three. Then *balancé* left toward center of circle, again swishing flags in an over top arch to left. Steps are left, right, left, sustain count three.

Lift us to the joy divine.

> Turn only one *pump turn* to right with flags held high in "V," then go to original locations at end of *Stanza 1*, keeping flags held up in a "V," where two dancers return to their original positions in *chancel* from where they began this dance, and other three dancers travel to *transept* to get to their original positions.

PART III—Practical Areas Regarding Liturgical Dance

Stanza 4
Mortals, join the happy chorus,

> *Transept dancers* and *Chancel Dancers:* On *"mortals,"* all dancers do a *relevé* step up onto ball of right foot suspended one-half tilt turn to right as flags are tilted over to right, the right flag is very low pointed to ground, left flag is held high to left, both at 180 degrees of each other, followed by two additional steps in same direction of tilt on *"join the."* On *"happy,"* all dancers do step up onto ball of left foot suspended one-half tilt to left as flags are tilted over to left, the left flag is down low, right flag up high at 180 degrees, followed by two additional steps in same direction on the word *"chorus."*

Which the morning stars began;

> All dancers: On third tilt, do full double *tilt turn*, same direction as first one-half tilt, ending with flags up in a "V" facing front. This full double-tilt turn is really several small quick steps taken on raised up on balls of feet with feet close together as you continue turning with flags.

Father love is reigning o'er us,

> *Transept dancers* face back, *Chancel dancers* face front: All dancers do slow "X" with flags starting from top with straight arms, coming down across front of body crossing to make an "X" then bringing flags out to sides then returning up to high "V" at top.

Brother love binds man to man.

> Both groups do one-half turn to right to face opposite direction and repeat *line three* of this stanza doing a second slow "X" movement returning up to high "V" at top.

Ever singing, march we onward,
Victors in the midst of strife;

> *Transept dancers* begin their exit out of the *sanctuary* down the center *aisle* toward the *narthex* by doing the following step with center *transept dancer* beginning the exit; then other two *transept dancers* following her out,

Choreography for Liturgical Dance

first dancer to right, then dancer to her left. Allow five feet in between dancers for recessional space. *Exit step*: *Triplet* step forward with flags swishing to right (right, left, right, sustain count three), then 3-step *triplet turn* to the left traveling forward with flags held high in "V." The two *chancel* dancers are doing this same step while traveling in a circle in a clockwise circle direction in *chancel* awaiting their turn to exit *sanctuary* in this recessional *sanctuary* exit. *Chancel* dancers must continue their traveling circle in the *chancel* until their turn to exit following the *transept* dancers by the end of lines five and six of this stanza.

Joyful music leads us sunward
In the triumph song of life. Amen

*Chancel dancer*s begin their *recessional* down the aisle following the *transept* dancers, first one, then the other, repeating the *triplet* step forward beginning right foot and *triplet turn* left beginning on left foot down the aisle. Dancers continue out of the *sanctuary* with same step until all dancers have exited the *sanctuary* and entered the *narthex*. If music ends prior to all dancers completing their exit from sanctuary, dancers continue exit into *narthex* walking with high flags.

PART IV

Shared Experiences of Liturgical Dance

CHAPTER 14

Interviews with Clergy, Church Musicians, Dancers, Choreographers, and Others Who Have Experienced Liturgical Dance

THE FOLLOWING ARE INTERVIEWS from a variety of individuals who have experienced liturgical dance firsthand through their involvement in the collaborative process. They are musicians, clergy, visual artists, dancers, choreographers, choir directors, and laity. Their comments are insightful, experienced, and extremely helpful to anyone interested in learning more about this worship art. I am grateful for their time in sharing heartfelt feedback through these interviews that helped me see dance with fresh eyes.

What is Liturgical Dance to You?

Joye Brannon, former Associate Pastor of Music and Worship, First Baptist Church, Greensboro, North Carolina

"A new way of having God speak."

Pastor Charlie Zimmerman, retired Pastor, First Lutheran Church, Greensboro, North Carolina

"Liturgical dance is one way we respond to, interpret, or experience God's Word. As David danced before the Ark,

PART IV—Shared Experiences of Liturgical Dance

and as there is a sense of dance in the Psalms, so God's presence, love, and Spirit set our feet to dancing. Life itself is a dance with God.

Liturgical dance is one means through which we can both give expression to our faith as well as involve our sensory responses in worship."

Anne M. Saxon, President, North Carolina Chapter of the American Choir Director's Association, Winston-Salem, North Carolina

"It is truly the externalization of the sacred word; the visual manifestation of *scripture in movement*. It speaks volumes and evokes feelings and emotions."

Jeannette Hassell, former Minister of Music, The Episcopal Church of the Holy Comforter, Burlington, North Carolina

"A dramatic stirring of space that quickens the soul and enriches the sacred mindset being sought."

Rev. Stephen Crotts, Minister, Director, Carolina Study Center, Chapel Hill, North Carolina

"Liturgical dance is color pageantry, costume, dance, drama, music and scripture incarnate. It is a tasteful means of proclaiming Jesus Christ in worship."

Rev. Courtney Jones Willis, Minister and Liturgical Dancer, Greensboro, North Carolina

"The first word that comes to mind is "freedom." Liturgical dance has enabled me to find freedom in prayer, in worship, and in praise. I have found freedom in using my body in worship and communication with God. I am free from sitting still, bowing my head, and closing my eyes in order for that worship and communication to happen. I am able to move and engage my entire self, body, and soul in that experience. I am free of the restraints we put on ourselves. Cultural, denominational, and social expectations are no longer an issue when using movement of whatever fashion in worship."

Interviews

Jane Cain, Director of Music, Davidson College Presbyterian Church, Davidson, North Carolina

> "Liturgical dance expresses the inexpressible, just as music does. It goes beyond words. Sometimes it makes you think about the words in a new way."

Anita M. Davis, Liturgical Dancer and Dance Educator, Burlington, North Carolina

> "Liturgical dance means communication with wings, a way to feel closer and more connected to others in the church, and a new language for prayer."

Dan Callaway, Professor of Music, Greensboro, North Carolina

> "Liturgical dance has been an amazing experience of worship in my life. I think that in one sense it took the focus off of the dancing and onto the *why*. In my experience, it was one of the most perfect ways to say "thank you" to God for the gift of a healthy body that can be awkward and funny, and at the same time, stunning and beautiful."

Ingrid M. Murphy, Liturgical Dancer and Dance Educator Princeville, Hawaii

> "As a performer of liturgical dance, my main purpose is to glorify God. God has given me this wonderful gift, the ability to dance. I feel I should absolutely use that gift in His honor. Liturgical dance makes me feel *whole* spiritually. I am passionate about dance and I am passionate about my faith. It just makes sense to me that the two should be connected."

Dr. Tom Henderson, Certified *Interplay* Leader, Raleigh, North Carolina

> "It may be that dance has the greatest capacity to move people deeply and correspondingly to frighten because it touches and reminds us of those experiences that are beyond the power of words to describe. It touches the mystery."

PART IV—Shared Experiences of Liturgical Dance

Bonny Buckley, Expressive Therapist, MA, LPCS, NCC, Thomasville, North Carolina

> "Dance is another way to express, to communicate, to share, to experience, to learn, to connect using the whole self—mind, body, and soul. Liturgical dance in my opinion is not necessarily better than other forms of worship, but it has the potential to add more depth. I am very aware that people learn differently—visual, tactile, auditory, etc.
>
> Liturgical dance means trying to reach out to more people. I admire Wellford's statement, 'somehow in the seeing, the sharing, the path is less lonely and there is immediate shared commonality.'"

What Makes a Dance of Worship *Sacred* to You?

Dr. Karen Josephson, New Haven, Connecticut, Performance Artist and Educator

> "Sacred dance is all dance that addresses any part of the entire gamut of the human condition and invokes God's participation in that condition, whether it is joy or sadness, wonder or despair. It may or may not happen within the context of a liturgy, ritual, or worship."

Rev. Dr. Stephen Shoemaker, Charlotte, North Carolina

> "Liturgical dance is sacred when it is performed with God as the first audience; when it draws the worshippers toward God and helps them say and feel what they most need to say and feel in God's presence."

Father Robert Benko, OFM Conv., Seaside, New Jersey

> "Something that you should not have to explain at its completion. Something that should speak to the experience of the people who are receiving this worship art."

Interviews

Rev. Scott Woodmansee, High Point, North Carolina

> "The strong feeling of the presence of God."

Jeannette Hassell, former Minister of Music, The Episcopal Church of the Holy Comforter, Burlington, North Carolina

> "It becomes *sacred by* our pre-set attitudes influenced by the context, the performers, the space, and the placement in the liturgy."

Bonny Buckley, Expressive Therapist, MA, LPCS, NCC, Greensboro, North Carolina

> "Dance in worship is sacred to me when the dancers are connected to the message they are trying to convey. They are not telling me the message, they are *showing* me the message."

Anita M. Davis, Liturgical Dancer and Dance Educator, Burlington, North Carolina

> "The dancer has to be capable of bringing the worshippers to a level of acceptance, to another plateau for prayer."

Eddie Huss, Minister of Music and Art, Shandon United Methodist Church, Columbia, South Carolina

> "It is *sacred* because it expresses our praise and thanksgiving to God. Dance may also enhance scripture readings or be an expression of prayer."

Pastor Charlie Zimmerman, retired Pastor, First Lutheran Church, Greensboro, North Carolina

> "The context and interpretation. When the movement and costumes fit the context of the word or music, it stirs my heart and conveys God's presence in a way that I might not have experienced otherwise. When it is done in praise, thanksgiving, or a way of honoring and glorifying God, then it becomes sacred movement for me."

PART IV—Shared Experiences of Liturgical Dance

Rev. Courtney Jones Willis, Minister and Liturgical Dancer, Greensboro, North Carolina

> "A dance of worship is sacred to me when it is a prayer. When I am removed from the performance aspect of dance and am focused solely on offering that movement to God as worship, and/or leading others to experience God in worship. Even if the performer is not feeling particularly "sacred" or invested, I believe others can still experience God through witnessing the movements. Dances of worship need not be perfect, or performed by professional dancers. If those who are moving are using the dance as a means of communication with God, it is sacred, no matter how pretty or technical the movements."

Is Liturgical Dance Affected by Location of Where it Occurs Such as a Sanctuary, Fellowship Hall, Stage, or Other Settings?

Wendy Wallace, Visual Artist, President of *The Christian Message Through Art!*, Greensboro, North Carolina

> "The advantage of being in a sanctuary is that the congregation is already primed for a spiritual experience. However, in a theatre or concert setting, the very "unpreparedness" of the audience may attribute to the success of reaching individuals' hearts."

Father Robert Benko, OFM Conv., Seaside, New Jersey

> "Regardless of where liturgical dance takes place, it needs to build a bridge to worship. Whether it takes place in the aisles or anywhere in the sanctuary or other places, it has to be done in a way that invites people to prayer."

Pastor Charlie Zimmerman, retired Pastor, First Lutheran Church, Greensboro, North Carolina

> "For me personally, the context and setting are important. I've seen ballet type movement danced both on

Interviews

stage as well as in worship. Either setting can be a sacred moment. It really depends more on what I bring and how I interpret what happens. I need to come with a sense of openness in body, mind, and spirit. I've been moved by sacred dance performed to contemporary music in a stage setting that was worshipful, as well as the more formal church setting."

Dr. Tom Henderson, Certified *Interplay* Leader, Raleigh, North Carolina

"I don't think it matters where it takes place. What *InterPlay* and sacred or liturgical dance both do is about connecting people at this very basic level, getting them in touch with the common humanity, and it is sacred."

Dr. Karen Josephson, New Haven, Connecticut, Peformance Artist and Educator

"Unfortunately, I do believe context influences liturgical dance, mainly from the perspective of the viewer. It is often more accepted outside the formal worship space, or in a more informal retreat type setting. Some dancers also feel permission when outside a formal worship service to offer things that might border more on the secular. I have never hesitated bringing the secular into sacred spaces, finding it a false division.

Therefore, in formal worship services, I have danced to *Fly Me to the Moon* and *The Impossible Dream* among others. I do not feel that "sacred" subjects, whatever they are, and movements (read angelic ballet) are the only ones appropriate for sanctuary dances. I have not yet been thrown out for my choice of tap, jazz, and choice of music."

PART IV—Shared Experiences of Liturgical Dance

Perceptions of Liturgical Dance: How Do You Feel Worship Leaders Perceive Dance in Worship Today? How Do You Feel Congregations Perceive Dance in Worship? Do You Think These Perceptions Are Valid or do They Need Enlightenment?

Dr. Karen Josephson, New Haven, Connecticut, Performance Artist and Educator

> "My experience in a wide range of congregations is that worship leaders are totally varied about dance in worship, some worrying about one lone dissenting voice in the congregation, and others plowing ahead ignoring the one crab. Worship leaders can also be wary of embracing moving bodies in worship which generally is a product of their past exposure to dance, and/or their seminary experiences."

Jeannette Hassell, former Minister of Music, The Episcopal Church of the Holy Comforter, Burlington, North Carolina

> "Worship leaders perceive dance as a new taste, a subtle but definite spice that awakens our senses. The congregation's perception is one of delightful surprise, a "peeling away" from the expected."

Father Robert Benko, OFM Conv., Seaside, New Jersey

> "I feel most priests might not want to incorporate liturgical dance within worship. Why? It is not because liturgical dance would not be a valid addition to the service. It is more about it being *one more thing* to worry about and include within an already busy schedule of multiple masses. Many priests have so many masses back to back. It takes time and collaborative effort to include *one more thing* in worship, even if it is a wonderful addition. I attended Washington Theological Union for my training and was exposed to many worship arts. I personally feel it is a welcomed addition to the mass. Liturgical dance,

when incorporated, needs to have collaborative effort and time to incorporate it effectively."

Ingrid M. Murphy, Liturgical Dancer and Dance Educator, Princeville, Hawaii

> "Most of the time worship leaders are very open to liturgical dance. Congregations are usually open as well. They view liturgical dance as a complement to the worship service. Both groups may have preconceived notions about liturgical dance if they have never seen it. Then, after they have witnessed it, they enjoy it and understand it better."

Have You Ever Experienced an Epiphany or a Revelation During or After Performing or Viewing a Dance of Worship?

Rev. Courtney Jones Willis, Minister and Liturgical Dancer, Greensboro, North Carolina

> "Once when I was leading a dance in worship workshop, I had an older woman come in the room in a wheelchair with an oxygen tank attached. My own insecurities ran rampantly through my head, wondering how in the world this elderly woman would be able to move and learn to worship with her body. She had a smile on her face. I began to cry as I watched her, ashamed of my misconceptions. However, I was taken aback by her willingness to move whatever she could and however she could to worship through movement. After teaching the class several postures, I played music and allowed them to improvise using these postures. I will never forget watching the elderly woman in the wheelchair, moving her arms and her head the best she could with the most peaceful, content, and proud look about her. It was her willingness to use her body, no matter how infirmed she was, to worship God with her whole self."

PART IV—Shared Experiences of Liturgical Dance

Have You Ever Felt One of the Following Viewpoints After Viewing or Performing a Dance in Worship?

> A. Liturgical dance is a conduit that enables others to connect and communicate with God more clearly within the worship service
>
> B. Liturgical dance is a distraction within the worship service.

Dr. Karen Josephson, New Haven, Connecticut, Performance Artist and Educator

> "I definitely believe A. I believe that through the arts, faith can be clearly understood and embraced, and it is through the arts that faith can most clearly be expressed. Images and senses go beyond words, the most common worship element. Dance, which often uses the art forms of music and/or well-crafted poetic words, penetrates the senses with three arts."

Ingrid M. Murphy, Liturgical Dancer and Dance Educator, Princeville, Hawaii

> "Most definitely I would agree with A. especially when a dancer gets positive feedback from the congregation. My favorite compliment was when a member of the congregation said, 'Thank you for leading me in worship.'"

What Was Your Experience Like Working in Collaboration with Dancers and Choreographers to Create a Worship Service?

Anne M. Saxon, President, North Carolina Chapter of the American Choral Director's Association, Winston-Salem, North Carolina

> "It was scary and thrilling all at the same time! Just to think that it is *a work in progress* and we are creating it to fit our music and our own worship space. I was surprised at how much the dancers themselves come wanting to

Interviews

get a worship experience out of it, as well as to do what they love. Our choir got to see that process in the finishing stages at the dress rehearsal, and it added an element of transcendence to the entire experience. Even the hired instrumentalists enjoyed it."

Wendy Wallace, Visual Artist, President of *Christian Message Through Art!*, Greensboro, North Carolina

"I had no idea how powerful liturgical dance could be! How heart wrenching and soulful movements on dancers' bodies can be to capture and transform the viewer. I was totally surprised!" Comments by Wendy Wallace following *The Life of Christ Celebration*, now *Celebrate, One Solitary Life!*, a huge collaborative worship service and stage presentation involving many forms of art about the life of Christ. Wendy was the producer of this huge collaborative worship arts venture.

For Dancers & Choreographers: How Do You Personally Prepare for a Dance of Worship?

Ingrid M. Murphy, Liturgical Dancer and Dance Educator, Princeville, Hawaii

A. "A dancer must be educated and well informed about the material (scripture, texts, and music) she is going to present. If study and analysis are not done regarding the material prior to the worship experience, the congregation will be able to see through vacant intention."

B. "As a dancer and performer, you must learn all the choreography and make sure to present the movement intended by the choreographer. It is *their* vision. Once the choreography is in your body, it becomes *yours.*"

C. "It is helpful to always pray before a worship service. Prayer enables you as a dancer to be centered and more connected with your intention. You should ask God to lead you through the service of worship."

PART IV—Shared Experiences of Liturgical Dance

D. "As a dancer, you must *always* have a spacing rehearsal."

Rev. Courtney Jones Willis, Minister and Liturgical Dancer, Greensboro, North Carolina

> A. "I listen to the music or read the scripture over and over again for quite a while to get the music engrained in my head. This enables me to think more clearly while choreographing the piece. I don't have to rely solely on the music to dictate the next movements. I can know where the music is going and where I can take the movements in regard to that knowledge."
>
> B. "Reading the scripture or the scripture the song is based on helps me to find movements that are appropriate for a specific dance. I generally spend a significant amount of time allowing this preparation to be part of my own worship, allowing God to use my body in the choreography and rehearsal process."
>
> C. "Generally, after allowing a great deal of time to consider the movements, music, or text in my head, I am able to create the dance smoothly and generally tweak it as I go."
>
> D. "I am very cautious to gauge the education of the congregation with whom I will be sharing in worship. If there is need for me to say anything before the dance begins, sometimes I may give an introduction. But in many situations, the congregation is already familiar with dance in worship and merely needs to experience the dance."

Dr. Karen Josephson, New Haven, Connecticut, Performance Artist and Educator

> "Prayer should be a component of the preparation, along with a healthy theology of the body and its ability to communicate. Practical issues vary, but dancers should feel "ready" in every aspect and in harmony with the rest of the service, the space, music, readings, etc."

PART V

Glossaries of Terms

GLOSSARY A

Terms for Liturgical Dance, Spatial Directions, and Dance Categories

Analysis—Detailed examination of elements or structure.[1] In liturgical dance, this might include contributory design and composition elements such as text, music, and movements.

Balancé—A waltz step shifting the weight from one foot to the other.[2] Balancé may be performed stepping to the side on one foot, rocking back on the other foot, then again stepping forward on the first foot. This rocking step is usually performed in three steps, taking three counts in waltz timing.

Choreographer—The designer or creator of the dance.[3]

Choreography—A term used to describe the actual steps, groupings, and patterns of a ballet or dance composition.[4]

Context—Parts that surround or clarify a word or passage; relevant circumstances.[5] In dance this might apply to what is expected of a

1. Jewell, *Oxford American Desk Dictionary and Thesaurus*, 27.
2. American Ballet Theatre's Online Ballet Dictionary; http://www.abt.org/education/dictionary/
3. Jewell, *Oxford American Desk Dictionary and Thesaurus*, 132.
4. American Ballet Theatre's Online Ballet Dictionary; http://www.abt.org/education/dictionary/
5. Jewell, *Oxford American Desk Dictionary and Thesaurus*, 164.

dancer when asked to perform a particular liturgical dance regarding where it is placed within the liturgy, or regarding the music or text of the dance.

Dance—An art form performed by individuals or groups existing in time, space, force and flow, where the body is the instrument and movement is the medium.[6]

Dance genres, or styles[7] *sometimes used within worship*—Ballet, modern, jazz, ethnic, contemporary, hip hop, tap, freestyle, fusion, signing, lyrical, folk, musical theatre, improvisation, pedestrian movements, and gestures.

Dance technique—The manner of artistic execution and artistry in dance; performing dance steps with skill and precision such as pointed toes, fully extended legs and arms, and clear focus.

Design—Plan, conception, arrangement or layout.[8] For dance, design might refer to the space where the dancer would perform within worship such as floor patterns, or physical areas such as chancel, aisles, or transept. The layout of the performance space may determine design and number of dancers to be used for a dance within worship. Design may also refer to the choreographer's use of dance choreographic elements.

Downstage—A term used usually in theatre settings where the dancer or actor would be located toward or at the front of a stage closest to the audience.[9] In most church sanctuaries this would be in the *transept* or crossing area, or the part of the *chancel* area closest to the congregation.

---

6. Kraus, *History of the Dance in Art and Education*, 24.
7. Jewell, *Oxford American Desk Dictionary and Thesaurus*, 335.
8. Ibid., 208.
9. Merriam-Webster Online Dictionary, http://www.merriam-webster.com/dictionary/downstage

Terms for Liturgical Dance

Elements of Dance—Body, Energy, Space and Time.[10] These are the basic elements from which dances are created. Choreographers use these elements in appropriate ways to bring well-crafted dances to fruition within various environments such as stages or worship sanctuaries.

 a. Body—Entire body of the dancer, making shapes, movements, and gestures while dancing. Some movements are traveling, others are stationary.
 b. Energy—Attack, weight, strength, and flow of the dancer while moving
 c. Space—Level (high, middle or low), direction, pathway, focus and size of movement
 d. Time—Speed, accent, duration, rhythm and dance combination or phrase

Fifth Position—An arm and foot position in ballet where both arms are raised over the head as if holding a tall crown on top of your head. The hands are generally about five inches apart in this position, never closed or touching. The dancer is standing with both feet turned out where the heel of the front foot is touching the toe of the back foot.

Fourth Position—A foot position in ballet where the feet are separated by approximately six inches, one in front, the other in back, turned out in opposite directions. This position is similar to *fifth position* except with six inches of space between the feet.

Plié—A bend of the knees.[11]

Postures and gestures for dance—The list below is from *Liturgical Danced Prayer* by Robert VerEecke[12] Portions in italics are from Jane Wellford.

---

10. Cornett, *Creating Meaning Through Literature and the Arts*, 297.
11. American Ballet Theatre's Online Ballet Dictionary; http://www.abt.org/education/dictionary/
12. VerEecke, "Liturgical Danced Prayer," 143.

GLOSSARY A

Standing—Primary attitude of respect

Sitting—Attentiveness, ease, comfort for listening, reflecting

Kneeling—Humility, penance, servitude

Bowing—Sign of reverence and respect

Prostration –Dramatic surrender, penance, unworthiness; *body is lying on floor*

Genuflecting—Same as kneeling

Joining of hands—Communal unity

Embracing—Love, peace, healing

Blessing—Grace and graciousness, sign of cross or open palms, arms extended

Striking of the breast—Contrition, mercy

Praying—Specific gestures with arms extended or hands clasped together; *reverence and honor to God*

Laying of Hands—Empowerment, healing; *touching another with your hand, most often on the head or shoulder*

Lunge—*A way of showing honor, extending upper body forward like a bow, arms down*

Turning of the body—Change of focus to another significant action; *continuation, eternity; a half-turn could mean repentance, or a change of direction and attitude*

Processing—Journeying toward

Pump Turn or Paddle Turn—Usually a repetitive turn in one direction where the feet are repeating a down-up version of quick foot work and the hands are often held in an upward "V." If turning right (clockwise), the dancer usually steps "down" on the right foot with a slightly bent knee, and then pushes slightly "up" on the left leg, doing this in a quick succession alternating weight while turning in a circle to the right, pivoting on right foot. The dancer does the reverse for a left pump or paddle turn going counterclockwise.

Terms for Liturgical Dance

Relevé—Raised; a raising of the body on the points or demi-pointes[13] of the foot.

Shape—To make external a form; to configure or give structure.[14] This might refer to the shapes the dancers are making in space with their bodies as soloists or as a group, or the overall shape of dancers in relation to their performance space.

Stage Left—As the dancer is *facing* the congregation from the center of the chancel or stage.area, this is the space to the dancer's left, the left side of the stage or chancel

Stage Right—As the dancer is *facing* the congregation from the center of the chancel or stage area, this is the space to the dancer's right, the right side of the stage or chancel.

Triplet—A dance step composed of three sequential steps in a forward or backward progression: down, up, up.[15] For example, step down *(plié)* on the right foot, step up *(relevé)* on the left foot, and then up *(relevé)* again on the right foot to complete the progression of this dance step.

Triplet Turn—Performing the step above while turning right or left, forward or back.

Tripudium Step—A processional step used in the late Middle Ages between the eleventh and twelfth centuries by early Christians. The symbolic meaning of the three steps forward and one step back reflects the following: Three steps forward signifies progress in health and welfare of the individual as well as the church and community; one step back signifies "setbacks" that all humans share.[16]

---

13. Miller, http://www.freedocsfile.com/doc-file/classical-ballet-terms-and-definitions-george-mason-univrsity

14. Jewell, *Oxford American Desk Dictionary and Thesaurus,* 766.

15. Modern Dance Technique, Language/Terminology, http://www.stolaf.edu/depts/dance/faculty/anthony/courses/Modern-Dance-Language.htm

16. Adams, "Communal Dance Forms and Consequences in Biblical

GLOSSARY A

Types of Dance Often Found in Worship:

Interpretive Dance—To interpret means "to explain the meaning of" or "to bring out the meaning of (creative work)."[17] The liturgical dancer's interpretation of their dance may be abstract or literal depending on the choreographer's choice. Interpretive dance may be accompanied by music, text, or performed within silence. Most dances of worship are interpretive dance in that they are the choreographer's interpretation of the text, the music, the choreographer's faith, or even her questions, all revealed through the dancer.

Liturgical Dance—A type of dance performed by a soloist or group of dancers, professional or non-professional, where the focus and intention is to worship God. Liturgical dance is often performed within a worship setting of a Christian liturgy, but may be performed in any location. It may also be seen within secular dance settings. Types of dance genres used for liturgical dance vary and may include ballet, modern, contemporary, jazz, hip-hop, ethnic, tap, signing, pedestrian movements, improvisations, or any style that is used to reflect the Holy, to praise God, or to express our human responses or questions to God.

Praise Dance—Dance used in worship or outside of worship to reveal joy, praise and celebration to God. Movements of praise dance are usually open, lively and larger in movement style than other types of worship dances.

Reflective Dance—Dance used in worship with the intention to cause the viewer to envision the dance content more introspectively when shared using this type of dance. *Reflective dance*, in contrast to *praise dance*, has a deeper, more dramatic dimension, and is sometimes slower and more graceful in its style. Reflective dance is often performed during the Christian church season of Lent to reflect Christ's suffering and crucifixion, or may cause the viewer to reflect upon other serious topics within worship.

Worship," 41–42.
    17. Jewell, *Oxford American Desk Dictionary and Thesaurus*, 435.

Terms for Liturgical Dance

Sacred Dance—The word *sacred* means "dedicated or set apart for the service or worship of a deity."[18] Sacred dance is dance that is holy or set apart for sacred purposes. Sacred dance may be used when referring to dances of worship in any faith tradition throughout the world. *Liturgical dance* is sometimes called *sacred dance* when speaking in terms of dance used in worship in general.

Symbolic Movement—Represented idea through expressive dance movement with the intention of conveying a represented symbol, idea, or thing through movement.[19]

Upstage—A term used often in a theatre setting where the dancer or actor would be placed in a stage location farthest away from the audience. In a church setting, the dancer would be the farthest from the congregation near the back wall of the chancel area.

Windmill arms—A dance movement of the arms; either on knees or standing, the dancer arches back and windmills outstretched arms alternately (right, left, right, left) similar to performing the backstroke in swimming. The movement is complete when the left arm ends reaching upward, the right arm is down, and facial focus is upward to ceiling.

Windmill roll turn with flags—Movement begins with flags held high, arms reaching upward from shoulders in a "V." If traveling right, bring right flag down across body to left as to begin a circle from left to right across body, continuing downward, then lowering left flag to follow the circle the right flag will be making. As the right flag is coming down across the body, dancer steps out to right on right foot which is the beginning of a three-step turn to right (right, left, right). After first step to right, both flags should be in a 180 degree straight line rotating with dancer's body as she turns on left foot now facing back, and then around on right foot to face front again. To complete, dancer brings right flag across

---

18. Merriam-Webster Online Dictionary; http://www.merriam-webster.com/dictionary/sacred

19. Jewell, *Oxford American Desk Dictionary and Thesaurus*, 849.

body again (standing stationary now) and joins it with left flag in parallel to make final additional circle going around right to end in a double parallel line of both flags about eighteen inches apart over to right upward diagonal where the dancer's focus will also be directed.

GLOSSARY B

Terms for Church Music

Anthem—A choral composition on a religious text, generally in English with organ, piano, or other accompaniment.[1]

Beat—Rhythmic pulse, such as the steady beat of a clock ticking.[2]

Coda—A concluding passage of a piece or movement of music.[3]

Cantata—Extended musical composition with vocal solos, choral group, and musical accompaniment such as organ or other instrumentation, or orchestra.[4]

Dynamic—Volume or relative loudness or softness of a sound.[5]

Hymn—Song of praise, especially to God in Christian worship.[6] The song may also be of lament, confession, a call to discipleship, or other subjects in singing to God.[7]

 1. University Society, *Pronouncing Dictionary of Musical Terms and Composers' Names*.
 2. Cornett, *Creating Meaning Through Literature and the Arts*, 347.
 3. Jewell, *Oxford American Desk Dictionary and Thesaurus*, 144.
 4. University Society, *Pronouncing Dictionary of Music Terms and Composers' Names*.
 5. Cornett, *Creating Meaning Through Literature and the Arts*, 347.
 6. University Society, *Pronouncing Dictionary of Musical Terms and Composers' Names*.
 7. VanderMeer, Organist & Director of Choral Music and Bell Choirs, Central Presbyterian Church, Atlanta, Georgia.

Interlude—A piece of music, usually brief, played between portions of a church service, or between stanzas of hymns.[8]

Measure—Beats *organized* within groupings of bars.[9]

Melody—The tune of the music; musical tones, or pitches falling into a recognizable pattern to make a musical theme.[10]

Meter—The basic pattern of accented and unaccented beats within each measure of a composition. The meter of a piece or section is indicated by the time signature, for example 3/4 or 4/4.[11]

Offertory—Usually a musical offering performed during a collection of tithes and gifts. This musical offering may be strictly instrumental, or in combination with singing of a choir, soloists, or congregation. At times, the offertory may be in collaboration with other worship arts such as liturgical dancers sharing in worship with musicians.[12]

Processional—Movement of worship leaders (clergy, choir, acolyte, and other worship participants) from the front doors of the worship space, down the aisles of the worship space, and into the chancel (pulpit) area. Often a hymn is sung by the congregation at this point.[13]

Recessional—Movement of worship leaders (clergy, choir, acolyte, and other worship participants) from the chancel (pulpit) area, down the center aisle of the worship space, and towards the

---

8. University Society, *Pronouncing Dictionary of Musical Terms and Composers' Names*, 48.

9. Ibid., 59

10. Cornett, *Creating Meaning Through Literature and the Arts*, 347

11. University Society, *Pronouncing Dictionary of Musical Terms and Composers' Names*, 60.

12. Murphy, Organist-Choirmaster, First Presbyterian Church, Burlington, North Carolina

13. Ibid.

Terms for Church Music

narthex and front doors of the worship space. Often a hymn is sung by the congregation at this point.[14]

Refrain—Repeated chorus; basic metrical unit in a verse, typically two to four lines.[15]

Rhythm—That aspect of music concerned with time and accent rather than pitch. The movement of music in patterns as subdivisions or combinations of a basic pulse or beat.[16]

Stanza—Basic metrical unit in a poem or verse, typically of four or more lines.[17]

Tempo—The speed, how fast or slow the music is.[18]

Timbre—Quality of tone or tone color; regarding music and its sound.[19]

Time Signature—How many beats there are in each measure, and what type of note gets a beat. The numbers of the time signature appear on a piece of music right after the key signature at the beginning of the music. The number on the top represents how many beats are in one measure of music. The number on the bottom represents what type of note gets one beat within the measure of music.[20]

---

14. Ibid.

15. University Society, *Pronouncing Dictionary of Musical Terms and Composers' Names*, 82

16. Ibid., 85.

17. Jewell, *Oxford American Desk Dictionary and Thesaurus*, 815.

18. Cornett, *Creating Meaning Through* Literature *and the Arts,* 347.

19. University Society, *Pronouncing Dictionary of Music Terms and Composers' Names*, 106.

20. Ibid.

GLOSSARY C

Terms for Church Sanctuary Spaces

Aisle—The open path walking area between pews or sitting areas.[1] This area, which may sometimes have steps, allows worshippers to enter and exit the sanctuary space.

Altar—A table, usually of wood or stone, on which the Eucharist is consecrated.[2]

Chancel—The part of a church sanctuary space near the altar and contains seats for the clergy and choir.[3] Worshippers in a church sanctuary are usually facing this area where the worship leaders and choir are leading the service.

Church –Building for public worship[4]

Communion Table—A table in the chancel or transept area of a church sanctuary where the elements of Holy Eucharist (bread and wine, or juice) are placed until served to the members of the congregation during communion.

---

1. Jewell, *Oxford American Desk Dictionary and Thesaurus*, 19.

2. Episcopal Diocese of Texas; http://www.epicenter.org/church-terminology/#Altar

3. Merriam-Webster Online Dictionary; http://www.merriam-webster.com/dictionary/chancel

4. Jewell, *Oxford American Desk Dictionary and Thesaurus*, 133.

Terms for Church Sanctuary Spaces

Crossing—In gothic church architecture, the main intersection of aisles at the front of the church. If viewed from above, these aisles form a large cross.[5] In this crossing area between the nave and the chancel, sometimes called *transept*, there is space to walk and there are usually no chairs or pews (see *transept*).

Narthex—A vestibule leading to the nave of a church.[6] The front entrance area of a church.

Nave—The central part of a church from the narthex to the chancel flanked by aisles. The congregation sits in the nave during worship services.[7]

Pew—Long bench with a back.[8] These are generally found in traditional churches for use of seating people and are usually located in the nave of a church sanctuary.

Pulpit—Raised platform area in a church, from which the preacher or worship leader stands to deliver a sermon.[9]

Sanctuary—Holy place, church, temple; house of worship.[10] Many churches or worship centers have one set place where communal worship takes place that is separate from the church education building or other satellite buildings. This location is usually called the *sanctuary*.

Transept—(See also *crossing*) The part of a cruciform church that crosses at right angles to the greatest length between the nave and the apse or choir.[11] In gothic church architecture, the main

---

5. *Episcopal Diocese of Texas;* http://www.epicenter.org/church-terminology/#Crossing

6. Merriam-Webster Online Dictionary; http://www.merriam-webster.com/dictionary/narthex

7. Episcopal Diocese of New York; http://www.dioceseny.org/pages/275-church-terminology#nave

8. Jewell, *Oxford American Desk Dictionary and Thesaurus,* 618.

9. Ibid., 673.

10. Ibid., 739.

11. Merriam-Webster Online Dictionary; http://www.merriam-webster.

intersection of aisles at the front of the church. If viewed from above, these aisles form a large cross. In this crossing area between the nave and the chancel, there is usually space to walk and there are usually no chairs or pews.

---

com/dictionary/transept, and The Episcopal Diocese of Texas; http://www.epicenter.org/church-terminology/crossing

GLOSSARY D

Terms for Christian Worship and Church Personnel

Acolyte—One who assists a member of the clergy in a liturgical service by performing minor duties[1] such as a lighter of the candles within worship or other assisting duties.

Church Seasons—Within the Christian church, there are seven seasons: *Advent, Christmas, Epiphany, Lent, Easter, Pentecost,* and *Ordinary Time.*

Clergy—The body of all persons ordained for religious duties.[2] Examples: minister, pastor, priest, bishop, etc.

Crucifer—One who carries a cross, especially at the head of an ecclesiastical processional.[3]

Deacon—One of the laypersons elected by a church with congregational polity to serve in worship, in pastoral care, and on administrative committees.[4] A deacon often acts as an assistant to a priest

---

1. Merriam-Webster Online Dictionary; http://www.merriam-webster.com/dictionary/acolyte

2. Jewell, Oxford American Desk Dictionary and thesaurus, 139.

3. Merriam-Webster Online Dictionary; http://www.merriam-webster.com/dictionary/crucifer

4. Merriam-Webster Online Dictionary; http://www.merriam-webster.com/dictionary/deacon

or minister.[5] A deacon is usually chosen and/or voted into position by the members of a congregation.

Elder—Often a mature and experienced layperson set apart by ordination to assist the minister in her/his administration and government of the church; elders were to set the example of a virtuous and godly life, and of regular attendance at public worship; to take part with the minister in the care and spiritual discipleship of the church. An elder is usually voted into position by the members of a congregation.[6]

Eucharist—Christian sacrament commemorating the Last Supper in which bread and wine (sometimes juice) are consecrated and consumed.[7]

Laity (or laypeople)—the people of a religious faith as distinguished from its clergy;[8]

Lectionary—In Christianity, a book or listing containing portions of *The Bible* appointed to be read on particular days of the year in Christian or Judaic worship.[9] Typically, a lectionary will go through the scriptures in a logical pattern, and also include selections which were chosen by the religious community for their appropriateness to particular occasions.

Liturgy—Prescribed form of public worship;[10] From Greek word *leitourgia* meaning "public service of the people."[11]

---

5. Jewell, *Oxford American Desk Dictionary and Thesaurus*, 192
6. Richardson, *Dictionary of Christian Theology*, 108.
7. Jewell, *Oxford American Desk Dictionary and Thesaurus*, 270.
8. *Merriam-Webster Online Dictionary*; http://www.merriam-webster.com/dictionary/laity
9. *Online Encyclopedia Britannica*, http://www.britannica.com/EBchecked/topic/334414/lectionary
10. Jewell, *Oxford American Desk Dictionary and Thesaurus*, 485.
11. *Merriam-Webster Online Dictionary*; http://www.merriam-webster.com/dictionary/liturgy

Terms for Christian Worship and Church Personnel

Minister or Pastor—A person whose job involves leading church services, performing religious ceremonies such as marriages, and providing spiritual or religious guidance to other people; a member of the clergy in some Protestant churches.[12]

Order of Worship—A set outline or rubric for the progression of worship.

Priest—Ordained clergy of hierarchical Christian churches.[13]

Prophet—A member of some religions such as Christianity, Judaism, and Islam, who delivers messages that are believed to have come from God; one who utters divinely inspired revelations.[14]

Religion—An organized system of beliefs, ceremonies, and rules used to worship a god or group of gods.[15] In Christianity, the religious practice is monotheistic, where only one God is worshipped.

Rite—A religious or solemn observance, act, or procedure.[16]

Ritual—Prescribed order for performing rites;[17] a formal ceremony or series of acts that is always performed in the same way.[18]

Rubric—An explanation or set of instructions at the beginning of a book, a test, etc. a rule for conduct in a liturgical service;[19] worship

---

12. *Merriam-Webster Online Dictionary;* http://www.meriam-webster.com/dictionary/minister

13. Jewell, *Oxford American Desk Dictionary and Thesaurus,* 656.

14. *Merriam-Webster Online Dictionary;* http://www.merriam-webster.com/dictionary/prophet

15. *Merriam-Webster Online Dictionary;* http://www.merriam-webster.com/dictionary/religion

16. Jewell, *Oxford American Desk Dictionary,* 723.

17. Ibid., 723.

18. *Merriam-Webster Online Dictionary;* http://www.merriam-webster.com/dictionary/ritual

19. *Merriam-Webster Online Dictionary;* http://www.merriam-webster.com/dictionary/rubric

services often have a prescribed order or bulletin with directions for worshippers to follow the ritual or worship.

Sacrament—Symbolic Christian ceremony or rite such as baptism or Eucharist; Sacraments involve or imply a promise or a commitment.[20]

Spiritual—Of or concerning the spirit as opposed to matter; religious, divine, inspired.[21]

Theology—The study of God and God's relation to the world; the study of religious faith, practice, and experience; a system of religious beliefs or ideas[22]

Worship—Reverence, devotion, or homage to a deity;[23] may involve attitudes and actions proper within a worship setting such as prayers, ceremonial readings, interpretations, songs, or dance.

Worship Committee—A group of laity and/or clergy within a church who are responsible for assisting with maintaining, and/or developing new ideas to include in worship.

---

20. Richardson, *Dictionary of Christian Theology*, 300.
21. Jewell, *Oxford American Desk Dictionary and Thesaurus*, 805.
22. Merriam-Webster Online Dictionary; http://www.merriam-webster.com/dictionary/theology
23. Jewell, *Oxford American Desk Dictionary and Thesaurus*, 971.

Bibliography

Adams, Doug. "Communal Dance Forms and Consequences in Biblical Worship." *Dance as Religious Studies*, edited by Doug Adams and Diane Apostolos-Cappadona. Eugene, OR: Wipf and Stock, 2001.

Adams, Doug, and Rock, Judith. "Biblical Criteria in Dance: Modern Dance as Prophetic Form." *Dance as Religious Studies*, edited by Doug Adams and Diane Apostolos-Cappadona, Eugene, OR: Wipf and Stock, 2001.

American Ballet Theatre Online Ballet Dictionary. http://www.abt.org/education/dictionary/index.html.

Bauer, Susan. "Dance as a Performance Fine Art in Liturgy." *Dance as Religious Studies*, edited by Doug Adams and Diane Apostolos-Cappadona. Eugene, OR: Wipf and Stock, 2001.

Bryans, Nena. "Arts in the Church: A Theological and Pedagogical Rationale." *Alert Magazine*. May, 1996. Vol. 26, No. 1.

Buttrick, George Arthur, editor. *The Interpreter's Dictionary of the Bible, An Illustrated Encyclopedia, R-Z*. Nashville, TN: Abingdon, 1962.

Cohen, Selma Jean, *Modern Dance: Seven Statements of Belief*. Middletown: University Press, 1966, Quoted in "Criteria in Dance: Modern Dance as Prophetic Form," *Dance as Religious Studies*. Edited by Doug Adams and Diane Apostolos-Cappadona. Eugene, OR: Wipf and Stock, 2001.

Confucius. *Chinese Proverb* attributed to Confucius.

Cornett, Claudia E. *Creating Meaning Through Literature and the Arts, 2nd Edition*. Saddle River, NJ: Merrill-Prentice Hall: 2003.

Erkert, Jan. "Modern Dance Technique, "Language/Terminology." Dance Center of Columbia College, Chicago, IL: *Online Terms and Definitions*, www.stolaf.edu/depts/dance/faculty/anthony/courses/Modern-Dance-Language.htm

Gagne, Ronald. "The Place of Movement in the Liturgical Prayer of Today," *Introducing Dance in Christian Worship*. Thomas Kane, Robert VerEecke, and Ronald Gagne. Washington, DC: The Pastoral Press, 1984.

Bibliography

Gruber, Mayer I. "Ten Dance-Derived Expressions in the Hebrew Bible." *Dance as Religious Studies*. Edited by Doug Adams and Diane Apostolos-Cappadona. Eugene, OR: Wipf and Stock, 2001. Originally published in *Israel Dance*, 1980 15-21, and Expanded for publication in *Biblia* 62/3 in 1981.

Hassell, Jeanette. Minister of Music, Episcopal Church of the Holy Comforter, Burlington, NC. Online interview, 2010.

Jewell, Elizabeth J. editor. *Oxford American Desk Dictionary and Thesaurus, Second Edition*. NY: Oxford University Press, 2002.

Kassing, Gayle. *History of the Dance: An Interactive Arts Approach*. Champaign, IL: Human Kinetics, 2007.

Kerrigan, Sheila. *The Performer's Guide to the Collaborative Process*. Portsmouth, NH: Heinemann, a Division of Reed Elsevier, 2001.

Kline-Chesson, Kathleen. "The Living Word: Dance as a Language of Faith." *The Christian Century*, March 22-29, 1989.

Kraus, Richard, Hilsendager, Sarah Chapman, and Dixon, Brenda. *History of the Dance in Art and Education, Third Edition*. NJ: Prentice Hall, 1990.

McBride, Richard, Chaplain Emeritus. Elon University. Elon, NC. Online interview, 2010. *Merriam-Webster Dictionary and Thesaurus Online*. www.merriam-webster.com.

Miles, Margaret. "Image as Insight." Beacon Press, 1985; *Alert Magazine*, May, 1996, Vol. 26, No. 1. "Arts in the Church: A Theological and Pedagogical Rationale" by Nena Bryans.

Nelson, James, B. *Embodiment: An Approach to Sexuality and Christian Theology*. Minneapolis, MN: Augsburg, 1978.

Olsen, Charles M. "Hands," *Presbyterian Survey*: 1969, Volume 59, Page 15. Published by Presbyterian Church in the United States, 1969. Digitized on August 11, 2009.

Project Dance, New York, NY. *Project Dance Foundation* internet website, 2010 and 2014. http://www.projectdance.com/?page_id=2. Permission to use quote granted by Cheryl Cutlip, Director of Project Dance, 2015.

Reeves, Betsy. Moving Liturgy Dance Ensemble dancer and Associate Director. Interview, 2004.

Richardson, Alan. editor. *Dictionary of Christian Theology*, Philadelphia, PA: Westminster Press, 1969.

Rock, Judith. "Dance Texts, and Shrines," *Dance As Religious Studies*. Edited by Doug Adams and Diane Apostolos-Cappadona. Eugene, OR: Wipf and Stock, 2001.

Saxon, Anne M., President of North Carolina Choir Director's Association, Winston-Salem, NC. Online interview, 2010.

Strong. *Strong's Concordance*. http://biblehub.com/greek/3009.htm.

Taussig, Hal. "Dancing the Scriptures." *Dance as Religious Studies*. Eugene, OR: Wipf and Stock, 2001.

Bibliography

Taylor, Margaret. "A History of Symbolic Movement in Worship." *Dance As Religious Studies*. Edited by Doug Adams and Diane Apostolos-Cappadona, Eugene, OR: Wipf and Stock, 2001.

University Society, Inc. *Pronouncing Dictionary of Musical Terms and Composers' Names: A Quick and Convenient Source of Information on Musical Meanings and Pronunciations.* Midland Park, NJ: 1976.

VanderMeer, David. Definition shared in 2013 from peer review reading of this manuscript.

Verhulst, Kari Jo. "Full of Grace and Truth: The Power of God in the Creative Vocation," *Sojourners Magazine.* May-June 1996, pp. 16-18.

West, John. Director of Valyermo Dance Company. Woodland Hills, CA; Comment from Panel Discussion on Sacred Dance, Sacred Dance Guild Festival, 2003, Scripps College, Claremont, California. John West attributed this quote to Father Vincent Martin, a Belgian Benedictine Monk from St. Andrew's Abbey, Valyermo, CA in the late 1970's.

Zimmerman, Pastor Charlie M., First Lutheran Church, Greensboro, NC. From a thank you note, 1991.

Zondervan. *The Holy Bible, New International Version.* Grand Rapids, MI: Zondervan Publishing House, 1988.

www.ingramcontent.com/pod-product-compliance
Lightning Source LLC
Chambersburg PA
CBHW060604230426
43670CB00011B/1965

* 9 7 8 1 4 9 8 2 3 0 0 6 3 *